EARN SAVE SPEND GIVE

Victoria,
To your
abundance
♡
Denise

DENISE HUGHES

EARN
SAVE
SPEND
GIVE

4 things to do with your money and how to make it all work

MONEY SCHOOL PRESS

Money School Press
www.denisehughes.org

First printing 2013
Printed in the United States of America
20 19 18 17 16 15 14 13   1 2 3 4 5

ISBN-13: 978-0615891125
ISBN-10: 0615891128

Library of Congress Cataloging-in-Publication Data
available upon request

I dedicate this book

to my mom, Julia, and dad, Jim.

They taught me that true joy is created from love

and our connection with one another,

rather than our accumulation of things.

CONTENTS

ACKNOWLEDGEMENTS

Many people supported the birth of this book.

I have gratitude beyond measure for my husband, Greg Hughes, for being my life partner and for being willing to confront our money demons as a couple. It wasn't always easy to work through our blind spots together, but our love was the glue that let us dive deep into our dysfunction and come out the other end more evolved people. I am proud of us! We are a great team, and we are rich in things money can't buy!

Heartfelt thanks to my soul sister, Patty Buch, for holding the dream for this book for years. She created graphic images of this book being on the *New York Times* best seller list as a motivator for me to write it and has always held my dreams as if they were her own. I love her dearly.

I thank B. Michelle Pippin, my business coach and midwife of this book. When I first started working with Michelle, she didn't know this book had been on the back burner of my life for years. With no blood flow going to it, it was a lost dream. Then out of the blue, during one of our business sessions, Michelle said, "Denise, I think we should stop what we're doing and change course. My heart tells me we need to move in the direction of you writing a book—that's the direction I think we should move forward in." And so we did. And the dream got birthed through Michelle's loving hands!

Thanks also to my amazingly gifted editor, Jennifer Read Hawthorne. Jennifer's skill is beyond words, and I have tremendous gratitude for her. Without Jennifer, this book would not have come together.

And I thank my clients, who stand naked before me, financially speaking, for all that they've taught me and shared with me. It is through working and helping each of them that I've gotten to go deep into the psyche of money—a place where I love to hang out and explore.

Last but not least, I thank other financial professionals, coaches, and mentors who have shared their expertise to support my growth and learning. If it hadn't been for Karen McCall of the Financial Recovery Center in San Anselmo, California, I'm not so sure our marriage would have survived. After working with Karen (as one of her couple clients), she suggested I'd be good at Financial Coaching. She planted the seed and it took root! In my heart I am forever grateful for Karen, her teachings, her wisdom, and for the contribution she made to my life and our marriage.

INTRODUCTION

Do you feel like you're suffocating financially? Does there never seem to be enough money? Are you tapping into home equity lines of credit, depleting retirement accounts, or going deeper into credit card debt to pay bills and monthly expenses? Have you created a financial plan with your financial planner but can't seem to stay on it?

If you said yes to any of these questions—or experience any kind of financial stress in your life—then this book is for you. Written for working mainstream America, *Earn, Save, Spend, Give* is about the nuts and bolts of building your financial foundation and how to overcome the pitfalls you may encounter along the way.

In this book we'll look at how you can manage your money, reduce and eliminate debts, save money for the here and now as well as your future, and ease financial stress. And although this book does not contain investment advice, we'll also focus on how you can save for your future years.

In these pages is the culmination of thirteen years supporting clients in developing a healthy relationship with money. They had the courage to look within to change their financial course— and they are living proof that it *is* possible to get a grip on your financial reality!

Why it Matters

Money is a blessing and great resource in our lives. Yet most people don't give money its proper "due," preferring instead to relegate it (how it is earned, saved, spent, and given) into a realm of mystery or chance, therefore lessening their personal responsibility for their "money matters."

And money does matter. It determines where we (or our children or grandchildren) can go to school, the neighborhood we live in, and how much we travel and experience in life, as well as other issues, such as health care and retirement options for ourselves and our loved ones.

If we are to reach our heartfelt hopes and dreams, we must steward and manage our money properly. Money management done "right" brings the habits of consciousness, clarity, prioritization, and, most important, planning to our financial house, helping our money last throughout our lifetime and possibly for generations to come.

Yet our family and educational systems fail to teach us life money management skills and behaviors that create a solid financial foundation in our lives. For many of us, we learn how to make money work through trial and error. And, as many of you know from personal experience, when money isn't working in our lives, financial anxiety and pain invite us to explore new ways of being with and handling money.

I See It. I Want It. I Buy It.

When I graduated from high school, I knew how to write a check. Later on, I was taught how to reconcile my checkbook with my bank statement "to the penny." My mom and I shared names on my bank account so she could "keep an eye on how I was handling money."

I learned meaningful money concepts from my Depression-era parents. Their unified approach to money was, "Live within your means," "Pay cash for everything," "Save some of your money every month," and "If you can't afford it, don't buy it."

There was something missing, however. It was the "how" part of implementing these concepts. I lacked skill in basic monthly planning of cash flow. I didn't realize the proper flow of money should be earn, save, spend. My mindset was spend what you want and, if there's anything left over, you can save. Unfortunately, nothing was ever left over.

I also thought everything was a need. I could rationalize every one of my wants into a need. Basically, I was managing my finances with my mid-brain, the part of the brain we share with the animals. This part of the brain likes to have fun—pleasure is its goal. The mid-brain's mantra is: "I see it. I want it. I buy it."

My frontal lobe, the planning, executive-functioning part of my brain, was asleep, financially speaking. The frontal lobe is where discernment lives, along with the weighing and measuring of consequences, setting priorities, and higher levels of thinking.

Fast forward a few years. I relocated from my Pennsylvania roots to California, where I met my husband, Greg. We both worked at Stanford University Hospital in the heart and lung transplant unit as registered nurses.

Our days off were spent having fun. Hiking in Yosemite National Park, lavish trips to the Sonoma coast, and road trips exploring the West were funded by credit cards. When we got married, we put our honeymoon on a credit card—$10,000 worth of fun!

We rationalized these credit card expenses by telling ourselves, "We have good jobs and can pay this off. We deserve this because we work hard." In all our fun, we didn't think about how we were purchasing the here and now with future income that wasn't in our hands yet. Credit cards gave us the illusion we had more to spend than we really did.

In our early years of marriage we dug ourselves deeper and deeper into debt. Out of control, we let life-insurance policies lapse, cashed out our Stanford IRAs, and deferred payments on things until our bills became debts. We had the newest electronic gadgets in our beautiful rented town home and books of photographs of the places we traveled together.

But neither of us were up to date on dental care. And I remember not having a winter coat for cooler weather. We consistently funded our wants over our needs, and the result was a deep, growing experience of deprivation.

Financial stress started to create stress in our marriage. Money leaked into every conversation in the way of "how are we going to pay for (fill in the blank)?" We no longer talked about our dreams because we could no longer fund them. We felt as if all we were doing was working to pay bills. Life wasn't fun anymore.

Hitting Financial Bottom

Finally we reached a breaking point. Our relationship was on the brink of divorce over our inability to manage money. We both suffered physical stress symptoms in our bodies. Anxiety, despair, fears, and worry began taking up more space in our lives. We both felt dead spiritually. We had hit our bottom.

Many people blame money for breaking up a marriage. But money doesn't break up a marriage. What breaks up a marriage is a couple not knowing how to talk about money, how to prioritize expenses, funding wants before needs, lacking a skill set in cash flow planning, and living in the blind spot of limiting money beliefs.

And we were guilty on every count.

When I look back and connect the dots that facilitated us hitting a financial bottom, here's what was really going on.

First, we weren't living in integrity. We said we wanted one thing (retirement savings, no credit card debt), but we were behaving in ways that created more debt, cashing out our retirement accounts to make ends meet.

We tried to keep cash flow number calculations in our heads. This didn't work very well. Our income/expense gap kept growing—in a negative way. We didn't have a visual tool or way to view money to help us make better choices. Nor did we know where to begin.

We both were re-creating the unhealthy family dynamics we had grown up with. I became the enabler and caretaker of our finances. I paid the bills, employed robbing-Peter-to-pay-Paul strategies, and carried the emotional weight of our financial secrets. My husband had a "hands-off" approach and a deaf ear when it came to our money. He avoided the bills, didn't look at the numbers, and, every time I brought up a conversation about money, said, "Can't we talk about something else? Why do you want to ruin a perfectly good day?"

We financed wants before needs. Funding surface wants while ignoring deep needs created for each of us a state of emotional, financial, and spiritual deprivation. The avoidance, arguments, unhealthy communication patterns, and overwhelming tension created a growing gap between us.

But we were so in the middle of our problems, we couldn't see what we were creating. A great quote by Albert Einstein comes to mind here: "No problem can be solved from the same consciousness that created it."

An Invitation

Money is a portal that invites us to enter the doorway to greater financial consciousness and self-awareness. Our portfolios, bank accounts, and financial struggles are mirrors reflecting back to us the behaviors we bring to our relationship with money.

My husband and I had many mirrors reflecting back to us, trying to show us that what we were doing and how we were thinking about money wasn't working. These mirrors reflected back for a long time before we took action and started to create a new financial picture. (You'll be able to read about how we turned things around in part 2. I'll also share a great tool for getting out of debt in the toolbox in part 3.)

The good news is that each of us can create the financial picture we desire. When we bring the right skill set and mature money behaviors to our financial lives, we change our course of direction. These changes, over time, support us in creating our hopes and dreams.

Earn, Save, Spend, Give will help you make these changes. In part 1 we'll look at:

- **Your relationship with money.** If any financial aspect of your life is not working well for you, understanding your relationship with money is the first step to learning what you can do to change things for the better.

- **The high cost of financial stress.** It's normal to feel resistance to making changes in your life—especially financial ones. But if you're finding it hard to get started, it may help tremendously to understand what you're likely to face down the road if you don't do something now.

- **Needs and wants.** Before you can put into action the new way of managing money, which we'll explore in part 2, it's imperative to understand the difference between a want and a need. You will be amazed at the changes in your life that happen when you begin to see the distinction.

Then, in part 2, we'll explore the four things to do with your money to make it all work:

- **Earnings.** Earnings are one of our greatest power tools and resources. But did you know you can earn as much or as little as you want? This chapter will answer questions such as: How do you create wealth? Are you earning enough? How much is enough?

- **Savings.** Saving money has become a lost art. As a culture, we're saving less and spending beyond our means. This chapter looks at three major reasons to save money first, then invest.

- **Spending.** Do you plan your spending? What if you knew that doing so would actually help you get more of what you wanted? This chapter addresses ways to get a handle on your income/expense ratio, and explores the neuroscience of spending—a window into how and why we make spending decisions.

- **Giving.** In this chapter, we'll look at ways to start giving and making a difference in the world. Giving "keeps the flow going," and it's your job to use it and give it wisely. We'll also offer some guidelines for "healthy" giving in this chapter.

At the end of the chapters in part 2, I'll share "pearls of wisdom" from successful financial planners and advisors I know and trust. I hope you find these pearls helpful and inspirational and that they light a gentle fire under you to motivate you to action!

In part 3, you'll find all the tools you need to make the changes you want in your financial life. These include:

- Your Financial Health Assessment
- Vision Board Tool
- Earnings Tool
- Spending Tool
- Get-Out-of-Debt Tool
- Gratitude Tool

The tools will be there for you whenever you need them. You may want to use some of them repeatedly. The Financial Health Assessment, for example, is a tool I recommend you use once a year to make sure you're on the road to meeting your goals.

Throughout the book I'll share stories about clients to illustrate and make practical the concepts being discussed. Please note that client names have been changed for privacy, and some stories represent a composite of clients.

May this book help you to EARN, SAVE, SPEND, and GIVE wisely, while your dollars nourish your deepest values.

Part 1

YOUR RELATIONSHIP WITH MONEY

Chapter 1

YOU AND MONEY

What adjectives would you use to describe your relationship with money? Would you say it's close, connected, fragile, estranged, shifting, complicated, unstable, the best of friends, at arm's length, not on speaking terms, rocky, loveless, or getting along famously?

However you'd describe it, there's probably good reason for the way you feel about money. The important thing is that if the financial aspect of your life is not working for you, you need to understand your relationship with money and learn what you can do about it.

For many of us, our relationship with money comes with lots of unconscious baggage, projections, and conflicting beliefs programmed in early childhood. Early influences carry great weight. These influences create the filters through which we view money, and they're responsible in part for our current money picture—unless we've done our inner work to clean up limiting beliefs, unhealthy money habits, and negative feeling states about money.

In this chapter, we'll look at the significant childhood influences that affect us as adults in our relationship with money. We'll also explore how to uncover the limiting beliefs about money that hold us back and keep us in an unhealthy relationship with the green stuff. Finally, we'll learn how to "talk" with money and transform our relationship with it into a powerful, positive experience.

Childhood Influences

One of the strongest influences shaping our relationship with money originates from our internal experience of whether our needs—and some of our wants—were met in our formative years. This influence is a foundational base that helps explain why we live from either a place of abundance or scarcity in our lives. What's surprising is how siblings with the same parents, growing up in the same house, can have different beliefs about money.

I once worked with two sisters who lived together. They were four years apart in age. They had parents who believed in fairness to the penny—what one child received, the other also received in time. So why were their adult views so different?

Jill's money memory was one of there never being enough in the family, while her sister, Emily, had the memory of there being more than enough. Maybe it had to do with Jill being the firstborn and her parents being tight with money when they first started out. Or perhaps Jill was more sensitive to the words "No, we can't afford that" than her sister. While Jill stopped asking for what she want and needed—because she believed she already knew the answer to her request—Emily never stopped asking and always received more, based on her continued asking.

Another strong influencer shaping beliefs comes from each of us witnessing how our parents or caretakers engaged with one another over finances. Think back. Did your parents talk about money in a normal tone of voice? Or was there tension when they talked about money? Did they work as a team, sharing decision making when it came to how money was spent? Or were there power struggles over money?

We often take on behaviors that mimic one or both of our parents' money management styles, even though we vow never to repeat the financial roles they modeled. We say things like, "I'll

4

never be a tightwad like Dad," or "I'm not going to spend away my retirement like Mom did."

Growing up in my family, I watched my mom pay the bills and handle all the finances. My dad earned the money, and that was the end of it for him. He handed all the money over to my mom, and then, when he needed money, he'd say, "Julie, give me some money." He would also frequently ask my mom if we could afford this or that.

I observed early on, even though I couldn't articulate it at the time, my mom and dad setting up a sort of parent-child dynamic with money management. My dad earned. My mom paid the bills, saved for longer-term goals (like our college education), and made sure money went where it needed to go to make our household run. My mom was also the one who communicated whether we could afford things or not (because she was the one in the know with the numbers).

These kinds of early influences are significant. Messages we receive with the innocence of childhood eyes and ears become internalized (in the cells of our being), because we believe in the absolute authority of our parents. These early messages are the beginnings in creating our subconscious beliefs, which we spend the rest of our lives acting out.

We repeat parts of our family behavioral patterning around money as we grow up. Some patterns may be healthy and work for us. Others may not work so well. These patterns can really come alive when we enter into relationship with another person. We bring our patterns, they bring theirs—and the marital money dance begins.

In my marriage, I subconsciously took on my mom's role in managing money. She was "hands on," and so was I. My husband subconsciously took on the financial modeling of one of his parents, which was "hands off." My husband would frequently ask me, "Can we afford this or that?" Déjà vu. This dynamic recreated the parent-child money dance for us—which both our parents had waltzed to.

Other influences exist as well. The culture, religion, generational influences, media, and the era we grew up in influence us. The Great Depression influenced my parents in more ways than I can share. They throw nothing out to this day, because "you never know when you might need it." Saving money remains a priority for them in their eighth decade. They pay cash or don't buy the item. They don't trust financial systems. The Great Depression influenced their lives so much that they continue to live as if another Great Depression is right around the corner.

Uncovering Our Money Beliefs

What beliefs have you internalized through the eyes of childhood that are ruling your financial life today? Most of us have one or two core beliefs that rule our relationship with money— and rarely are these beliefs based in reality. Here are examples of common limiting money beliefs. See if you can relate to any of them:

"If I have more money, it will change my personality to the dark side."

"I should be taken care of financially."

"If I get in a jam, someone will always pay my way out of it."

"I don't have time to manage my money. Life is too busy."

"Having money makes me feel guilty when others have less."

"I am more comfortable living broke. I don't do so well when lots of money comes my way."

"In order to have money, I have to work hard for it."

"It is better to give than receive."

"Rich people can't be trusted."

"I deserve to get what I want when I want it. Life is short and you can't take money with you."

"If I become rich, something will happen and all of the money will be taken away from me."

Another limiting belief was experienced by Leslie, a client of mine who initially came to see me because she was deep in credit card debt for the fifth time. When I asked her what her thoughts were as to how she might begin to get out of debt, she told me, "I could get married again, and my new husband could take over paying my debt off for me." She wasn't dating at the time.

I immediately observed that her solution to tackling her debt was based outside herself. She wanted "someone to take care of her debt for her." In digging deeper, Leslie uncovered the desire to be rescued financially for most of her life. Her ex-husband, dad, serial boyfriends, and several credit cards were all part of the team that had rescued Leslie. She often stayed in relationships with men even when the love had dried up—just for the money.

This wore at her self-esteem. Her desire to be rescued financially was interfering with her growing need to live a life of integrity. But this inner conflict also spurred her into making the choice to stand on her own two feet financially—for the first time in her life.

Thoughts, Feelings, and Actions Behind Money Beliefs

When I help a client uncover their core money beliefs, we plot out on paper their thoughts, feelings, and actions supporting the belief. Thoughts, feelings, and actions are the three components that make up one's behavior, and behavior is the blood flow that keeps the belief alive.

Here is a visual to help you understand how money beliefs are created, which begins with how we are programmed from an early age:

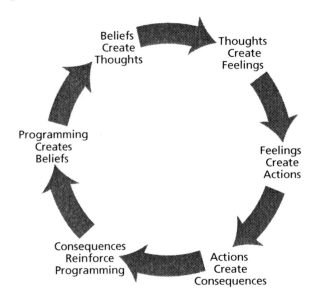

Two of Leslie's core money beliefs were, "I deserve to buy whatever I want, whenever I want," and "I shouldn't have to manage my money; someone should do that for me." You can tell these beliefs have roots in early development, somewhere between toddlerhood and adolescence, because developmentally they lack the quality of accountability.

Leslie's thoughts supporting this belief were: "If I want something, I should be able to buy it regardless of what is in my bank account," and "If I need money until my next paycheck, I can take a cash advance or find someone to give me money."

Leslie's feelings supporting this belief were "deserving, entitlement, wanting to be taken care of."

Leslie's actions supporting this belief were spending without knowing the amount of money available in her bank account, resistance to creating a spending plan for fear of not being able to get what she wanted, and placing expenses on her credit card so she didn't have to deal with not being able to get what she wanted when she wanted it.

Of course, over time, our behaviors create consequences. These consequences can be positive, moving us toward our goals, or negative, distancing us from our deepest desires. In Leslie's situation, her behaviors created the consequences of mounting credit card debt, depleted investment accounts, a drop in her credit score, a neglectful relationship with her money, and a lack of confidence in her ability to manage money.

When limiting money beliefs are present, so are distancing and avoidance behaviors. These behaviors create a Teflon coating with money. It's as if the dollars themselves know they are not welcome to hang out in our orbit or our bank accounts.

Usually, the first place we look to change things is our outer circumstances. We believe the answers and relief we need are found in divorcing our partners, claiming bankruptcy, selling our home, serial refinancing, bleeding our long-term investment accounts, asking family for a loan as a temporary life jacket, or finding another rescue strategy to give ourselves breathing room.

The problem is that when we look outward rather than inward for change, our outer circumstances continue to repeat themselves over and over again, until one day we awaken to the real work that needs to be done. This work is "inner work." This work is about understanding, healing, and transforming our relationship with money.

My Personal Financial Crash

I too looked outward for solutions to my own financial situation, thinking that cashing in one more IRA would solve the problem of my husband and me overspending. After my IRA was cashed out, the next rescue strategy was credit cards. After my credit cards were maxed out, I asked my parents for money.

It was a scary time. I was running out of rescue strategies. I remember the day of desperation when I called my parents and asked them for a loan. Crying, I told them we owed the IRS $3000.

My dad first asked me if I had credit card debt. I told him I did. I then listened to him tell me in a loud voice how credit cards were the ruination of our country and how he didn't believe in them. He never agreed to help pay the loan over the telephone, yet told me he would be sending me something to help me.

A few days later a package arrived from him, beautifully wrapped. I opened it on Christmas day; it was a pair of silver scissors. The note read:

Dear Denise,

Cut up your credit cards. Start learning to live within your means. I'm not being mean. I want you to learn how to live in the world and depend on yourself. You won't be able to do this if we rescue you.

Love, Dad

I cried when I read his note. I felt hurt and angry that my parents were opting out of being a part of my financial rescue strategy. I also understood the lesson they were trying to get across.

Shortly after that, my husband and I entered into financial counseling. This process was the beginning of us looking deep within to our relationship with money, as a couple and as individuals.

It took us a few years to get ourselves back on track, out of debt, and able to save money for the here and now, as well as our future. We didn't create our mess overnight, and we didn't clean it up overnight. But the understanding, healing, and transformation that came from this process were truly priceless. We wouldn't be where we are today without it.

We've made money work in our lives with job losses, illness, and the unexpected curveballs that life sometimes throws. Through all of it, we still live life without a credit card. This is something we are very proud of and wouldn't have been able to accomplish unless we had done our inner work.

Money Dialogues

One of the best ways to begin exploring some of our dominant beliefs about money is to enter into dialogue with it. Olivia Mellan, co-author with Sherry Christie of *Money Harmony: A Road Map for Individuals and Couples* (scheduled for publication in 2013) and a pioneer in the field of financial therapy, shared this exercise with me. It's profound, fun, and ever so revealing. Here's what you do.

Imagine you and Money are sitting in comfy chairs facing one another, in a quiet private space where you can talk openly and honestly. Allow Money to begin the conversation with an opening sentence of inquiry or observation relating to your mutual relationship. What would Money say about being in relationship with you, for example?

Then you answer back. Then Money answers back. Do this for about three lines of dialogue each.

Add in one-line commentaries about this dialogue from significant people in your life—your mom, your dad, and your Higher Self (which could be God, the Universe, or any higher energy). See what unfolds.

Here are two examples of money dialogues I did when taking a class with Olivia. I'm so addicted to doing money dialogues that I now do one every week.

Denise's Money Dialogue #1

Money: Why do you think you have to work hard to have me?

Denise: It's all I've known to be true about you—that you come through *hard* work. And I don't want to work harder. I'm fifty-five years old and want you to come to me effortlessly.

Money: I am easier than you think ... all you have to do is to ASK for me more, invite me in ... get the "hard" out of your mindset. Think "flow," like a river, NOT "hard," like a rock. I like it better that way too ...

Denise: You think you're so smart.

Money: I am smart; so are you. I'm right here at your door ... now open it with ease.

Commentary

Husband: This is "woo-woo."

Mom: What you're saying doesn't make sense to me.

Dad: (No words, just a shake of his head with disapproval.)

Universe: They don't know me like you do. You know my true nature. They told you lies about me. Let the lies go. Now you know me and we can do our own thing ... our new song is flow, flow, flow ... stay open to receiving, Denise.

Denise's Money Dialogue #2

Money: I like it when you look at me each month to see if I'm growing or shrinking. This makes me feel like you're paying attention to me.

Denise: I worry that you aren't going to grow enough to support me in my old age. I want there to be enough of you.

Money: It's important for you to remember that if there isn't enough of me, you always find a way to get your needs met. You are creative and resourceful, and your deepest needs are hardly ever met by me anyway.

Denise: I forget this sometimes. I forget that having "enough" for me is really about loving my life, my work, and all the people in it. I do appreciate you, though, and all that you provide me with.

Money: Just keep watching me with soft eyes, Denise. I'll grow the best I can. No need to watch with vigilance and fear. That makes me as jumpy as it makes you!

Commentary:

Mom: Don't worry, dear, Dad and I are here to help you with anything you need.

Dad: Don't spend on anything that you can't eat or wear. You don't need that much money.

Universe: Denise, dear, knock, knock. Remember me? I am here for you in all ways … to guide you … to create opportunities for you to step into. Trust. So far, we've made it all work out magnificently, shifting from two incomes to one, dealing with life's curveballs …. There is nothing we can't handle or find a solution to, you and I—we rock!

Your Money Dialogue

Money:

You:

Money:

You:

Money:

You:

Commentary

Mom:

Dad:

Significant Other:

God, Your Higher Self, the Universe:

These dialogues are a beginning step in exploring the relationship between you and money. Each dialogue has the opportunity to bring you to a new level of understanding with your relationship with money, uncovering hidden internal conflicts you didn't know existed and patterns of behavior and attitudes that may be keeping you stuck in your money life.

For me, these money dialogues open me with insight to the blind spots I've been living in. One of the gifts in becoming aware of our internal dialogue is to then take different action than what we have been doing, in order to move us closer to the kind of relationship we desire to have with our finances. If you're willing to try them, these dialogues will begin to create a foundation of financial intimacy between you and money.

When you and money are more connected, you then have the opportunity to create a new relationship based on understanding and respect. You can forgive yourself for past misunderstandings about money and, once and for all, begin to shift out of the space of stress and struggle into a space of peace.

Chapter 2

THE HIGH COST OF FINANCIAL STRESS

Once you've freed yourself from financial stress, you'll likely never want to go back. But if you're having trouble getting started—trying to get a handle on your financial life but not feeling motivated to do anything about it—it may help you to understand the high cost of financial stress.

Financial stress can happen suddenly and unexpectedly. Job loss, divorce, illness, or the death of a partner can be a crisis that creates both an emotional and financial toll on us. In one fell swoop we can be dropped to our knees, confused about how best to move forward financially in a new life circumstance and fearing our most basic needs will not be met.

But MOST OFTEN, financial stress grows slowly and worsens over time. We succeed or fail gradually through the choices we make over days, months, and years. The consequences of our choices gain momentum over time. When Ernest Hemingway was asked, "How did you go bankrupt?" he replied, "Gradually, then suddenly." Isn't this the way life is? Habits over time create gradual results, positive or negative, and then reach a crescendo.

The slow, insidious nature of spending more than we earn, funding our wants over our needs, neglecting to learn how to manage our money, operating in unconscious blind spots

15

of limiting beliefs, and behaviors of avoidance with money eventually catch up with us.

It starts by living paycheck to paycheck, and in this chapter, we'll look at why and how that happens. We'll also address the symptoms of financial stress—the toll it takes on body, mind, and spirit. The cost is high, but recognizing the signs is the first step in reversing the trend.

Living Paycheck to Paycheck

The experience of chronic financial stress begins by living paycheck to paycheck—without a safety net to fall back on. One reason we get ourselves into this situation is that we lack clarity about how much money is coming in and how much is going out. Many people aren't able to tell me what their take-home pay is every two weeks or the cost of their lifestyle choices.

This lack of knowing regarding how cash flows in our lives is merely a lack of an emotional connection with our money. It's not to be judged or to have shame over. But it is important to realize that when we live in financial vagueness, we unconsciously spend money on things that don't offer us the proportionate value of the money spent.

An example of this is the Latte Factor, the term coined by personal finance guru David Bach to illustrate that the amount of money a person spends on a little thing, like a daily Starbucks latte and snack, can add up to a huge amount of money (in this case, close to $2000 per year). The point is that when we spend unconsciously, our bank accounts take a hit. And when money is spent first on unplanned non-essentials, available funds to pay for our survival needs in any given month begin to diminish.

Then a common scenario begins to unfold. We get one to two months behind in our regular bills. Some of these bills become debts. We use credit cards to bridge the income-expense gap. We get close to maxing out the cards. We ask for pay advances. We owe the overdraft account at our bank significant money. Checks bounce. Insurance premiums lapse. We feel out of control. There is lots of drama around money, and our money life isn't working very well.

(I feel as if I need to take a deep breath here just writing this. It brings back painful personal memories.)

Then we think of and act on more risky strategies to obtain money. We tap into retirement and investment accounts, taking out 401K loans. Home equity lines of credit get tapped. We may refinance our homes in order to pay off debt. Soon, monthly payments to credit cards, combined with other loans, leave us with barely enough money to meet our survival needs.

Band-Aid Strategies

Lack of connection with our money, financial vagueness, and superficial Band-Aid strategies to make cash flow work further create stress in our lives. Why? Because this lack of connection and consciousness creates an experience of living on a financial cliff without a parachute; it places us in an experience of survival and lack. The corner we've trapped ourselves in makes us feel out of control, scared, and hopeless.

Shame prevents us from talking about feeling out of control with our finances. We keep silent about what is going on inside our financial lives, while still looking good on the outside to our friends and family. And in doing so, we rob ourselves of any chance of getting the help we so desperately need.

Often, our first solution in dealing with financial stress is to earn more, thinking more money will solve our problems. Studies tell us that, in general, people believe if they earned fifty percent more than what they do, they wouldn't have money problems.

But earning more is rarely the full solution. Working more to earn more eats into our precious time and life energy. We miss important family events. We're too tired to give our best selves to our relationships. We get out of balance with ourselves, maybe eating more or drinking more to numb our anxiety.

We go deeper and deeper into a state of depletion and deprivation. Our physical, emotional, and spiritual well-being is compromised. Symbolically, we begin to live in the "red," a place of debt at all levels of our being. Living in this state is not sustainable.

Effects of Financial Stress on the Body

Chronic stress wreaks havoc with our cardiac, immune, digestive, and nervous systems—and more. While studies vary, some reports state that as many as 76% of Americans experience some form of financial stress.

A study done by Paul Lavrakas and Patricia Drentea from Ohio State University was one of the first to make a connection between credit card debt and health (*Social Science & Medicine*, February 2000). Many of the 1000 responders they surveyed who had credit card debt or worried about credit card bills reported anxiety, the inability to control their emotions, a loss of concentration, insomnia, and heart problems. They were also more likely to smoke and be overweight.

It's interesting to note that those with higher levels of debt experienced higher levels of physical impairment. The study also suggested that stress comes not only from the amount of credit-card debt one carries, but the internal shame people have that they spend more than they earn.

When our bodies get stressed, the hormones cortisol and adrenaline get released. These hormones are necessary to help the body in temporary emergency (fight-or-flight) situations by increasing our blood pressure, heart rate, and respiratory rate; they help us to be hyper-alert in order to protect ourselves. But when cortisol and adrenaline are chronically elevated in the body, we put ourselves at risk for chronic inflammatory diseases, including obesity, diabetes, heart disease, chronic fatigue syndrome, irritable bowel syndrome, and others.

When my husband and I were out of control spending and not managing our finances, I frequently had diarrhea and chest tightness, and I sometimes felt short of breath. He had gastric symptoms and increased irritability. We also suffered from headaches, tiredness, teeth grinding, muscle tightness, and insomnia.

Since the OSU study, many other studies have linked financial stress to bodily stress and illness. The MetLife Annual Study of Employee Benefit Trends from 2011, for example, found that employees that suffer from financial stress take more time off work, have decreased productivity from not being able to concentrate on the task at hand, and spend more money on medical care.

Such research has the ear of American corporations, because the financial well-being of employees ultimately affects the bottom line of their companies. As a result, some companies are putting holistic financial wellness programs in place to help employees get out of the paycheck-to-paycheck cycle, get out of credit-card debt, and apply basic financial knowledge to their lives.

The Effects of Financial Stress on the Mind

Money problems create mental stress as well. We lose our focus; instead of paying attention to the task at hand, like driving our car, our mind wanders, figuring out how to pay bills or how to deal with creditor calls.

This is what happened to me. I remember getting speeding tickets every month because I daydreamed about financial worries when driving. Thank goodness I didn't hurt myself or anyone else.

Forgetfulness, lack of creativity, loss of humor, inability to make decisions, an overwhelming sense of pressure, and memory loss are all signs of mental financial stress. Can you relate?

The worry created by mental stress can stop you from getting the sleep you need to be healthy and at your best. These are some of the stressful thoughts my clients have shared with me over the years that have kept them awake at night:

"I'm 60 years old and I don't have any savings. How am I going to retire? My younger self told me I'd want to work until I died and that I'd have the energy to keep going, going, going—but my younger self didn't know my older self when these assumptions were made. I don't have the energy I used to, and, quite frankly, time is now more important to me than money. And I have neither."

"I'm 48 years old, recently divorced, and I've been a stay-at-home mom my entire marriage. I don't know a thing about finances; that was my husband's job, and now I have to figure out how to "do money" in my life. HELP! I don't know where to begin."

"I am a high earner with no savings and growing debt. I've always been a believer of living in the present. You can't take it with you. I have two luxury cars, a home way bigger than I need, lots of chotchkies, and I don't

have money to pay the IRS my tax liability this year. I can't live this way anymore."

"We earn great money but it isn't enough. We need to save for our two kids so they can go to decent colleges. Our aging parents need help and we need to seriously start saving for our retirement so we aren't a burden to our kids. Lately, we've both been having anxiety over how are we going to do it all. (Silent scream!)"

As if the worry itself is not harmful enough, the resulting lack of sleep creates even more health problems. It's a vicious cycle that becomes very hard to break.

The Effects of Financial Stress on the Spirit

Financial stress affects our spirit as well. Anxiety, despair, depression, edginess, feeling powerless, being easily upset, crying, utter exhaustion, hopelessness, and depletion are all signs our spirit is overwhelmed.

When we reach this level of stress, we lose our glow, feel empty, and may even feel and verbalize that life is not worth living. A handful of people I've worked with over the years even told me they had had thoughts that their family would be better off living off the death benefit of their life insurance.

Then there's financial stress affecting our significant relationships. When relationships with our partners are healthy, they're a source of spiritual nourishment. But when dysfunction around money rears its ugly head, relationships can take on tension, and building resentments can harden once heartfelt connections.

Money can become the third party in the marriage, even in the bedroom. I can't tell you how many husbands have told me their wives bring spreadsheets and calculators to bed to have money conversations right before trying to go to sleep. This can ruin a couple's sex life and create a wedge of tension that breaks the bonds of connection, warmth, and intimacy.

When a couple can't talk about their money issues, honestly and at the appropriate time, it becomes the controlling party in the relationship. The result is nothing less than a deadening of the spirit.

Your Next Step

Whatever your financial situation, there is hope and help, even when you can't imagine a solution exists. For now, take some time to answer these important questions to gain insight about how financial stress is affecting your body, mind, and spirit. Sit in a quiet private space, take pen to paper, and be honest with yourself. What really speaks to you in this chapter?

- How is financial stress affecting your body? Your mind? Your spirit? Your life?

- How much longer are you willing to live with this stress? Why?

- What is your greatest fear in letting go of the pain you're in?

Identify what type of support you're willing to access in order to lessen the financial stress you're experiencing in your life. Some ideas are: read a book, take a basic finance class at your local community college, hire a coach to help you, begin reading one finance blog a day to expand your knowledge, or find and join an online financial community.

Chapter 3

NEEDS VS. WANTS

When you cannot distinguish between wants versus needs,
or if you can't identify a want as a want, you set yourself up
to live in a constant state of craving and disappointment.
—Anonymous

What if I told you your wants in life are a disguise, a superficial layer of your underlying true needs? Would you believe me?

Your entire effort to change your relationship with money, to make it all work for you, is dependent on understanding the difference between true needs and wants, so that you can get a grip on where your money is going and how to redirect it to support you on every level—financially, mentally, emotionally, physically, and spiritually.

When we spend wisely, money is the blood flow that nourishes our deepest values. When the deepest parts of ourselves are nourished and we feel fulfillment from the inside out, we experience a sense of enough in our world.

So what's the difference between a want and a need? It can be very confusing. How do we know a need is a need? How do we know we aren't rationalizing a want as a need? Are we even in touch with what we really need? Do we even know what we really want?

Let's explore this all-important concept as a basis for putting the principles in part 2 into action. In this chapter we'll discuss the five types of needs we all have, from physiological to psychological, and, most important, how to find ways to meet many of our needs without having to pay for them. This understanding will help tremendously when we begin to look at the prioritized steps of EARN, SAVE, SPEND, and GIVE in part 2.

Needs vs. Wants

Let me give you an example of how gaining clarity about your needs versus wants can change your financial life. Alex, a high-level, successful businessman in the tech industry, called me one day and said, "I earn well over $200,000 a year, and I don't have enough money to take a vacation. Something is not right with this picture. I can't understand how I can earn a lot of money and still be unable to do the basics things other people do. I haven't had a vacation in over five years, and I need one badly."

One of the first things Alex and I did was to gain clarity on where his money was going—how much was going to certain expenses and *why* it was going to those expenses. In tracking his numbers, both inflow and outflow, we discovered some very interesting things.

About $3000 a month was spent paying for other people's food and drinks at certain prestigious nightclubs in the San Francisco Bay area. Alex told me this was the normal custom that "We pay for each other and it all comes around." He also noticed a large amount of money spent on alcohol, about $500 a month.

Alex and I had several heart-to-heart talks about what he really wanted to create in his life and what he felt was missing. One reason he went to clubs was in hopes of meeting someone he could begin dating. He also confessed he was unhappy in his job; he wanted to find work that was meaningful and get out of the corporate rat race.

Once Alex began to identify his true needs—the need to connect and be in a relationship, finding meaningful work, having time off to relax and think about his next move, and spending more time in nature—we started to allocate dollars toward those needs.

First, he adjusted his club spending down to $500 a month and his alcohol consumption down to $200 a month. This gave him $2800 a month to begin saving for both a vacation and his job transition. Instead of looking for a date at a club, Alex joined the Sierra Club and started dating a woman he met during a hike. That same year, he took a vacation to Europe and thoroughly enjoyed himself. He also started a savings account, which he called his "screw you" account, which would support him once he decided to leave his current job.

Alex also made significant mindset shifts. He mustered up the courage to pay only for himself on club nights. At first, he blamed it on me and told his friends, "My financial consultant told me I need to allocate my money in different ways, and she cut out my generosity in this area." (Just to be clear, Alex came to this decision on his own as a result of tracking his expenses, looking at his numbers, and choosing more wisely for himself about funding his true needs.)

He also became aware of a long-standing pattern of behavior in his life, that when he was unhappy, he often medicated his unhappiness with alcohol or distracted himself by going out to clubs and settling for what he called superficial connections with people. Neither of these activities was really supporting the direction Alex wanted to move in his life.

Money works best for us when it is given a direction and

purpose. If you don't direct your money where to go, in a conscious way, it begins to leak and flow into areas of life that may not be worth that much value to you. And, before you know it, you will be having an experience of living paycheck to paycheck and feeling that there's never enough money.

More important, you will believe there isn't enough money, when the truth is that money isn't being allocated in a way to give you an experience of enough in your life. Many of us are out of touch with what our true underlying needs are. Once we identify those needs, however, our money can be the blood flow that nourishes them.

Survival (Physiological) Needs

Let's look now at the various types of needs we all have, so we can see first how to recognize them, and second, how to prioritize and fund them.

The Merriam-Webster dictionary defines a *need* as a physiological or psychological requirement for the well-being of an organism. In the 1980s, renowned psychologist Dr. William Glasser developed Choice Theory, which states that all human behavior is an attempt to satisfy five basic needs.

One of these needs is survival, a physiological need. The remaining four are psychological needs: power, love and belonging, freedom, and fun. Dr. Glasser believes that by understanding these five human needs, we are able to make better choices for ourselves and improve the quality of our lives.

Let's look at the first need, survival. Providing for our survival is a need that must be satisfied before all other needs. If we don't pay attention to funding our survival needs, we will eventually die. Food, clothing, a roof over our heads, and health care are survival needs.

26

Depriving ourselves of food over time will lead to cell death, organ death, then death of the organism. Clothing and shelter are important physiologically to protect us from the elements; without them, our bodies wouldn't tolerate the ice cold of a winter snowstorm or the scorching heat of the summer sun. Health care is a need as well. Regular dental, vision, and medical care help keep our bodies functioning at their optimum level of wellness.

It's important to note that while food, clothing, shelter, and health care are physiological needs that we all share for survival, we cannot fool ourselves into thinking that shopping at high-end retail clothing stores is a need when we can purchase more moderately priced clothing to serve the purpose at hand. We cannot fool ourselves into thinking that a Toyota will not serve the same purpose as a Mercedes or that an apartment, condo, or townhome won't serve the same purpose as a villa or mansion.

Whatever your income, you can find creative ways to get your survival needs met. Think functionality, not brand. And keep in mind that research shows our happiness quotient doesn't rise all that much after our survival needs are met. In other words, what we spend money on *beyond* our survival needs has been found *not* to bring us greater happiness.

Psychological Needs

Now let's look at the psychological needs we all share: power, love and belonging, freedom, and fun. Because we are each unique human beings, we are unique in the ways we get these needs met. But while the priority and intensity of these needs are unique to each of us, we often spend money on things in an effort to satisfy one or more of these psychological needs.

Let's look more closely at each.

Power

This is a need to feel important through accomplishment of some form. Some of us may get our power needs met by living a life of purpose and meaning, being at the top of our class in school, creating a buffed body in top shape, becoming famous, being a good employee, earning lots of money, or enjoying some other form of what we perceive as success.

When power needs are met internally—a person feels and experiences themselves in control of their life and environment—they spend less money. When a person does not have an internal experience of personal empowerment, they can spend money until the cows come home trying to purchase this need through "stuff" and experiences.

Brian, a client of mine who had been out of work as the result of a layoff, came to our session one day and told me, "I'm obsessed with wanting to get a large flat-screen TV for our home. I really need this. I've shopped around, researched the best quality through Consumer Reports magazine, and I'm ready to buy one."

When Brian and I talked about his true need and what was under the strong desire to purchase this TV at a time when he already had limited funds to live on, he said, "I feel 'less than.' I just want to be one of the guys and feel equal to my friends. They all have flat screens (this was when flat screens were newly out), and I want to buy one and have them over to my place so they can see I'm doing well too."

This was an "ah-hah" moment for Brian. A lightbulb of awareness went off in his brain as he understood that he got his power needs met mostly through his work accomplishments. I helped Brian take stock of other areas of his life where he had significant accomplishments—he was a great husband, his kids loved him, and he had great friends. And after we talked about this for awhile, he realized that a flat screen was a temporary fix to get his power needs met.

So Brian started a daily gratitude practice, in which he took stock of all he was thankful for every day. Instead of buying a flat screen TV, he contributed a case of beer whenever his friends called him over to watch sporting events on their TVs.

Digging deep to the underlying need below a surface want is important both to your bank account and your ever-growing state of consciousness with money. Brian saved money, and eventually, when he went back to work, he did get a flat screen TV. At the time of purchase, he also knew what *need* he was funding, which at that point was the need for fun. Working with Brian taught me how a want like a flat-screen TV can really be a way to satisfy different shifting needs at different points in time.

Love and Belonging

Our brains are wired for connection with one another. We are social beings who need positive, loving relationships in our lives to feel fulfilled. Loving relationships can create in us that warm honey feeling that all is well in our world. Positive relationships relieve stress in our lives and make us feel safe.

There's a difference between the need for "love" and the need for "belonging." Love is about a deep heart connection, a soulful partnership. Belonging is about being part of something bigger than ourselves, which can take the form of being a member of a group, a cause, a movement, or an organization.

Now, when we don't meet our love and belonging needs in ways of true connection—that is, spending time with people that matter in our lives, talking about what is going on at a feeling level, sharing both our joys and sorrows, and feeling safe to be vulnerable—it's possible that we'll try to fund this connection through money.

We might buy expensive, over-the-top gifts for people, thinking this is a true sign of love. We might pay top dollar to join a prestigious club, engaging in the superficiality of "nice" behavior while feeling empty and lonely inside. And, when we don't know how to truly connect with another human being, heart to heart, spirit to spirit, we may try to numb our loneliness by spending more money on alcohol, food, and other addictions.

One of my favorite stories about getting love and belonging needs met is from Steve and Carol, a married couple I worked with. One day, Steve walked into my office and announced he was going to buy a motorcycle—and he said it with strong conviction. In the six months I'd been working with Steve and Carol, I'd never heard Steve say anything about wanting a motorcycle.

We were just in the place of turning their financial picture in the direction they wanted. They were going to be completely out of debt in one more month. Their savings was on target. A motorcycle would definitely change some financial dynamics here.

When I asked Steve why he wanted a motorcycle, he said to me, "I've been thinking the only way I can get quality time with my wife is to have her close to me, hugging my waist, with just the two of us riding together out in the open with no distractions. A motorcycle will do this for us."

While this may have been true, Steve, Carol, and I talked about other ways they might deepen their connection. Carol agreed to let go of some of her volunteer activities to spend more time with Steve. They instituted a date night each week. They didn't have to purchase the motorcycle—it was no longer necessary to spend money on something that would falsely buy love and connection, when they could meet this need for much less money by creating quality time with one another in other ways.

Freedom

To me, freedom means living life on our own terms. No one enjoys being dictated to or living under someone else's rules. The need for freedom is why young adults can't wait to leave the nest of their parents' home. We each want the freedom to choose what we believe to be true, where to live, what we want to experience, whom we want to be in relationship with, and how to creatively express ourselves.

When our sense of freedom is cramped and we feel stuck in a corner with little to no choice, we spend more. I've witnessed clients and friends in unhappy marriage relationships where they've felt trapped. I've seen the despair that comes from being out of work, with multiple job application rejections and the feeling of being in a dead-end corner.

I think we can all relate to various times in our lives when we've lived in a corner and can't seem to find a way out. But while spending can give us a high and soothe the pain of the negative emotional state we may be in, like Prozac, it's only temporary.

When my husband and I were in a lot of credit card debt, we felt caged with no way out. In the beginning of our marriage, when we used credit cards to fund our need for fun and love, oh, we felt so free. And then came the responsibility of paying all that back to the credit card companies, which payments ate into our discretionary spending—and life wasn't all that free-feeling anymore. I remember that, during those times of being in a debt corner, I wanted to spend more money on stuff I didn't need.

Ironically, getting your financial life under control will actually create greater freedom than you've probably felt in a long time.

Fun

Life is meant to be enjoyed, isn't it? Life is better when we laugh, experience a light attitude, relax, and just be. We all need this. Our nervous system needs fun and relaxation on a regular basis to heal and restore itself.

When we are chronically overwhelmed, overworked, out of balance, and haven't given ourselves the pleasure of fun in our lives, we spend more. We spend more because we tell ourselves, "I deserve this or that because of how hard I work." Or I hear, "I haven't had a vacation in five years." Our body, mind, and spirit need time off on a regular basis.

I've noticed a tendency in myself and with my clients that being out of balance can justify bigger spending, sometimes spending proportionately to the amount of imbalance we are experiencing in our lives.

You see, our survival needs cost the most money, about 50 percent of our earnings. On top of that is saving money, which is also a survival need if you want to bring security to your future self when you're no longer working. I would suggest saving 15 to 20 percent of your gross earnings for the longer term. That leaves about 30 percent of your earnings to spend funding the other needs we just talked about.

Meeting Psychological Needs without Money

One of the secrets in my husband's and my life that has helped us to reach our financial goals is to find creative ways to meet our power, love and belonging, freedom, and fun needs spending as little money as possible.

Let me give you some examples. Here is how I meet my love and belonging needs. My husband and I take hikes and walks with our dogs each week at the ocean. Sometimes we don't even talk that much. We just enjoy being together as a pack, enjoying the sound of the crashing waves, sea smells, and the warm ocean breeze. We also love to plant a garden and to cook new recipes together and try them out on our friends. I belong to one organization, and that's enough for me.

I have women friends that I love and adore. I share things with them that I don't always share with my husband; my husband knows this and is thankful for my women friends. I love hiking with my friends, sweating and sharing conversations from the heart. These connections make my life feel full, bring me great joy, and make me feel supported.

My power needs are met when I feel as if I'm making a difference in the life of another. I do this by serving others through my business, as well as being the best nurse I can be when I do shift work at the hospital. I receive enormous satisfaction knowing that I have helped another, whether helping a client transform his relationship with money or holding the hand of a patient at the hospital to ease her anxiety.

I meet my freedom needs by staying conscious to what I let into my life and what I say yes to and what I say no to. I fully own all of my choices and take responsibility for the life I create. When I get frustrated and feel trapped, I examine the choices I've made to create that experience, learn from it, and promise myself to do better next time.

And when it comes to fun, I have fun each day in some form or another. Sometimes I listen to my favorite music, do yoga with a ball, play with our dogs, or cook fun dinners with my husband.

Yes, it costs money to fund our psychological needs, but it doesn't have to cost a lot if we're creative. For example, let's say you want to learn a new language for fun. You're going to Paris next year and want to learn French. You could take a French language class at a community college, study from a book, go to France early and take a language class in France, or buy some podcasts that teach you the basics. Each of these ideas will help you get closer to your goal; you just need to examine which choice is most friendly to your overall cash flow plan.

Remember, it costs a whole lot more money when you aren't aware of your true needs and you think that a superficial want will meet that need, like Steve's idea of a motorcycle.

Exercise

In what order of importance do you place your psychological needs of personal power, love and belonging, freedom, and fun? Place them in order here, with number one being your most dominant need and number four being your least dominant need.

1.

2.

3.

4.

5.

Now, list five ways you can meet each of these needs, and place a dollar amount next to each idea. See how much your true needs actually cost. Do they cost more or less than what you thought?

Here's an example of how it all works for me.

1. **Freedom** is my highest need. I am my own boss. I don't take direction well and like to do things my way. Here's how I get my Freedom needs met without spending money:

    - Choosing my friends wisely—$0.00
    - Choosing how I spend my time—$0.00
    - Choosing how I spend my money—$0.00
    - Choosing the right support for me—$0.00
    - Choosing how much I work—$0.00

2. **Love and Belonging** is second for me. I value my family and friends. It's important for me to cultivate healthy relationships where I can give and receive love, and honor and appreciate the value others add to my life. Here's how I get my Love and Belonging needs met without spending much money:

    - Taking walks with husband and dogs—cost is gas money to the beach
    - Having friends over for dinner—cost is buying food for enough people
    - Giving and receiving love and affection from my husband—$0.00
    - Hiking, sweating, and sharing conversation with my girlfriends—cost is an occasional pair of hiking boots and gas to drive to the hike
    - Talking to my parents on the phone almost daily— $15 month in phone charges

- Creating relationships based on love and healthy boundaries—$0.00

3. **Power** is a need I get met by making a difference in people's lives:

   - Being results- and process-driven in my Financial Consulting Business—$0.00

   - Feeling good about the lifestyle my husband and I have co-created—$0.00

   - Staying true to putting money away for our retirement savings—$IRS maximums allowed to a 401K

4. **Fun** is a need I continue to learn to embrace. Growing up on a farm, we worked before we played, and there was hardly ever any energy left at the end of a day to play. I notice I get cranky and irritable when I'm out of balance these days in work and play. Here's how I get my Fun needs met spending very little money:

   - Playing in my garden with plantings and design—$50 a month

   - Painting and decorating our home just the way we like it—$250 a month

   - Taking a day trip with my husband, our dogs, and cameras—$60 each day trip

   - Reading before I go to bed on my iPad—$50 a month for digital books

   - Committed to my yoga practice—$150/month

Exercise

Now it's YOUR turn. For one month, monitor your expenses. Ask yourself WHY you are spending money on each expense you incur, and identify what need you're meeting in your life with each. Are you purchasing a survival need, a personal power need, a need for love and belonging, a need for freedom of choice, or a need for fun and pleasure? What are you really buying?

Gain clarity here and you will come to a new and deeper understanding of the needs your "surface wants" are really trying to fill.

Part 2

4 THINGS
TO DO
WITH YOUR
MONEY

Chapter 4

EARNINGS

Your greatest asset is your earning ability. Your greatest resource is your time.

—Brian Tracy

If you want to make your money work, then the first thing we need to talk about is earnings. Earning money is one of life's great pleasures and necessities. As success guru Jim Rohn says, money isn't everything, but it ranks right up there with oxygen.

But did you know that you can earn as much or as little money as you want in your life? That's right—you read that correctly. The only thing that limits you from earning all the money you want is your own *internal* earning ceiling, lack of creativity, or failure to put your creative ideas into action. Even if you have a job where you receive a paycheck every month or every two weeks, it's possible to earn beyond your paycheck if you desire.

Our earnings are one of our greatest power tools and resources. Earning our own money is a developmental milestone, just like passing our first driver's test. When we begin to earn an income that sustains us, we begin to stand on our own two feet, financially speaking. We become the boss of the other three pillars of money management: how we SAVE, SPEND, and GIVE. We no longer have to ask our parents to give us money to fund our needs and wants. (Yes, I know many grown adults who rely on their parents for money.)

I clearly remember receiving my first paycheck years ago—the feeling I felt of both joy and responsibility, knowing that I would decide and choose how and what to allocate my earnings to. That first paycheck represented the scissors that cut the financial umbilical cord I had to my parents and the say they had over what I could do with money.

Did you know that earning, or "making money," is an American concept? There's a great quote from one of the main characters in the book *Atlas Shrugged*: "If you ask me to name the proudest distinction of Americans, I would choose—because it contains all the others—the fact that they were the people who created the phrase 'to make money.' No other language or nation had ever used these words before; men had always thought of wealth as a static quantity—to be seized, begged, inherited, shared, looted, or obtained as a favor. Americans were the first to understand that wealth has to be created."

So how exactly do you create wealth? Or at least enough to live comfortably and cover your wants and needs? What are the characteristics of high earners? How can you make money beyond your salaried job? Are you earning enough? How much is enough, anyway? And why do you want to earn more? Is it possible to earn enough without using credit cards as a source of income? And is it possible to have peace of mind when it comes to money?

We'll explore the answers to all these questions in this chapter.

Creativity vs. Credit Cards

Growing up on the family farm in southwestern Pennsylvania taught me lessons about earning. My dad worked in a steel mill and earned about $38,000 a year. My mom worked on and off at different secretarial jobs between raising her kids, with earnings of about $10,000 a year. My parents put all three of their children through college, totaling about $150,000 at the time, and they paid cash.

How did they do it? They were creative. Besides doing her secretarial job, my mom brought in extra money by teaching herself to bake specialty cakes for weddings and showers. She was the local "go-to" baker, known for cakes both beautiful and delicious.

My dad worked double shifts around the time our school tuition came due. He also collected scrap metal to sell and did odd jobs to earn more when the need for increased earnings arose.

My parents had a strong work ethic and earned money to pay for what they valued most: a basic lifestyle, yearly family vacations, and their kids' education. These were their top priorities, and the money they earned was the blood flow that funded their highest values.

There is something important to note here. When we close doors to financial rescue strategies (like credit cards and home equity loans) as income sources, we open ourselves to exploring the divine gifts we were blessed with. Our task then becomes using our divine gifts to serve others in the world. Because my parents closed the door to using credit as an income source, this spurred their creative juices as to how to earn more creatively. They used their innate talents and inner gifts to create enough money for their family to live on.

In my life today, I am very creative in how I earn the money I need and want to make life work, as is my husband. I have two revenues streams that feed my life, as does he (we are both creative types).

One of my income streams is working part-time as a registered nurse at a local hospital, which gives my husband and me the health benefits we need and contributes to the amount of money we need to make our cash flow work on a monthly basis.

My second revenue stream, my financial consulting business, is my "soul work." This stream helps fund our joint seasonal expenses (vacations, property taxes, annual insurance premiums, out-of-pocket medical, dental, vision costs, vet visits for our pets, taxes), fun, our longer-term retirement goals, and the expenses my business incurs in order to sustain and grow.

How you design your income streams will be unique to you, your gifts, and your needs.

Your Creative Gifts

How about you? Are you earning what you want to be earning? If not, why not? Is it because you define yourself by your job? And you think it's not possible to earn beyond whatever your job pays?

If so, it's time to rethink things. Because earning is about much more than your job—it has to do with getting in touch with your unique gifts and putting legs on your creative ideas. And it has no limits—except the ones you put on it.

First, ask yourself what you could do and what you'd be willing to do if you wanted to earn more money. It's also important to know WHY you want to earn more—your WHY is what motivates you. Having a desire or intention can begin to open us to new ways of bringing money in beyond our paycheck. Plus, it's rewarding to have a goal to work toward and then see it become a reality.

So what would be the reason for you to earn more money? Would it be to pay off debt, save more for retirement, fund your bucket list, pay for your children's education, engage in philanthropy, or increase your lifestyle choices?

When you get clear about *why and what amount* you want to earn, the universe will step into support you in unimaginable ways.

Once you know why you want to earn more, consider your skills and talents. We've all been blessed with special gifts, and it's up to us to figure out what they are and then offer them to the world. When we tap into that, we maximize our earnings.

What gifts have you been blessed with? Think about what you're really good at. And if you can't think of what you're good at, then think about what others compliment you on—this will possibly give you a clue.

Next, ask yourself how you can monetize your gifts as you serve others. When we use our gifts to serve, our payment is in the form of money *plus* the deep satisfaction of knowing our services helped another. This creates a healthy flow of giving and receiving.

Obstacles to Earning—and How to Overcome Them

Besides defining ourselves by our jobs, there are many other ways we stop ourselves from earning more. Over the last decade and a half of working with clients, I've witnessed many behavioral traits that stop people from earning to their potential. Here are the top five—and what you can do to avoid them:

1. Unwillingness to Risk Discomfort

This can mean not asking for a raise, trying something new to create a new revenue stream, increasing fees for existing and current clients, or taking the next important step to growing our earnings. High earners are just as uncomfortable as low earners taking risks. The difference is that high earners take strategic risks—and keep taking them—while low earners don't take action at all.

So feel the fear, say hello to it, invite it in for coffee—but not for dinner. Be willing to be uncomfortable taking risks you haven't taken before. Create a side business. Turn your hobby into a business. Or see if you can find a way to monetize your unique gifts.

2. Inherited Wealth

Inherited wealth frequently stunts a person's motivation to work and earn. Inherited wealth can be a blessing and a curse equally when it comes to earning money and standing on one's own two feet financially. When we're born with "enough" money, we frequently lack motivation to earn more.

This is mostly due to our survival needs already being met, as well as having enough money for wants and other needs—much the same way a wild animal who begins relying on humans for food loses its hunting instinct. And risks starvation if the food "given" to him runs out.

Here's how to turn an inheritance into a blessing (it's actually good advice for everyone). Create a vision your earnings can support. Your vision needs to be heart based so it motivates you to get out of bed in the morning. I don't know of many people who are willing to get out of bed for the sake of "making money." I do know that we will get out of bed to make money if we have a vision of what that money can create for us in our lives—something that is meaningful and enriching. Get in touch with what it is you want money to help you create or accomplish in your life and keep your focus on this.

3. Imbalances in Giving and Receiving

People that are better givers than receivers earn less, compared to people who are balanced in giving and receiving energy. Many times, people that over-give do so for approval from others or to people please. This can lead to expending lots of energy with a low return monetarily on one's investment.

Develop a ROI (Return on Investment) mindset when it comes to your time, energy, and money. High earners embrace this mindset. They are consciously evaluating whether their time and energy is a fair exchange of the money they receive in return. If it isn't, they do something about it. They are able to let go of what doesn't work and move on. They constantly re-examine priorities. Adopting these habits will help you become a smarter and more successful earner.

4. Not Valuing Your Divine Gifts

People who don't value their divine gifts or believe in their intrinsic value earn less than people that value what they bring to the table of life. When we don't value ourselves, we ask for less money—or don't ask at all. Rather than taking our place at the table of life, we sit on the outer perimeter.

The answer? Do whatever it takes to learn how to value your divine gifts, even if it means working with a counselor to do some deep emotional work.

5. Projecting Our Limiting Beliefs

When we project our limiting beliefs onto others, we earn less. Many of my clients are female entrepreneurs. When I work with them on growing their earnings, I often hear: "Clients won't pay me more than what I am already asking." "If I move my office, it will be too far for clients to travel." "My clients will leave me if I increase my rates."

When my entrepreneurial clients share their limiting belief mind chatter, I lovingly remind them that it's *their* internal limiting beliefs creating their reality. As business owners, if we don't work through our own limiting beliefs and charge what

47

the market will bear for our services and what we need to earn to sustain ourselves, we are doing ourselves and the world an injustice.

Again, it's imperative that you get help to change your self-perception.

Do you recognize yourself in any of these descriptions? If yes, then it may be time to do some deeper work with a financial counselor who understands the psychological needs component of making your money work. Removing these kinds of obstacles from your life will open the door to financial freedom, allowing you to go beyond surviving to thriving.

Self-Worth vs. Net Worth

You can be a high earner and still feel poor if you aren't making value-based spending decisions. Why? Because your money will be frittered away unconsciously on things that aren't really that important to you.

Know the difference between self-worth and net worth. Self-worth can increase a person's net worth, but net worth doesn't necessarily dictate self-worth. Mother Teresa had significant self-worth and very little net worth. Princess Diana had incredible net worth and worked hard to gain self-worth.

Money can buy us lots of things—but not everything. It can't buy love, hugs, smiles, friends, family, sleep, laughter, good memories, gratitude, a connection to God, satisfaction from making a difference in the life of another, or love from our pets, to name a few.

It's really important to know what it can and can't buy, so we can be careful not to throw money at things it cannot buy. And remember: money solves money problems. It does not solve emotional problems.

ASK for what you want and need in your life. That could be a raise supporting your level of contribution and performance, higher rates on services and products if you're in business for yourself, or help and support from others. Many of us, including me, were taught that asking for help is a weakness. But the act of asking is not a weakness. It is a strength to help us elicit support, ideas, and resources for what we want to create in our lives.

So flex your asking muscle. Who knows—you might get what you ask for!

How Much Is Enough?

How much is enough? This is the million-dollar question, isn't it? What is enough money? And how do you know if you're earning enough? The easy answer to this last question, of course, is that your earnings need to fund your survival needs (food, clothing, shelter, health care, transportation), some fun and recreation, and savings for BOTH the short- and long-term.

But "enough" money is a different number for each of us, which takes into account our lifestyle choices, values, and priorities. So one of the exercises I do with my clients is what I call a Bare Bones Spending Plan (you can do this for yourself in part 3).

This is a plan of no frills—just the basics. This is spending that would need to happen even if you were out of a job; it helps define the minimum amount of earnings needed to fund survival needs. Once we know what a person's Bare Bones Spending number is, we can work upward from that place.

Knowing this number helps in two ways. First, it helps people to know what pay-scale range to negotiate when looking for a salaried job or what amount needs to be earned if one is in business for himself or herself. The goal isn't to earn at this basic survival level; the goal is to know what your survival earnings number is and earn enough beyond that to include fun, adequate savings, and investment goals as well.

Second, it helps people to know the amount they'll need should they want to make a life transition. Knowing your bottom line earnings number can bring you peace of mind in times of life transitions.

Remember that your lifestyle is dictated by your earnings. One of the biggest problems many people run into is that they tend to fund their psychological needs—love, belonging, personal power, the freedom to choose, and fun—before their survival needs. For financial peace of mind, cover the basics first; a good formula is to use 50 percent of your earnings for your survival needs, 20 percent for savings, and 30 percent for everything else.

In our culture of MORE, we think earning MORE money is often the answer to life's financial problems. It is NOT. Managing our money is the solution to our financial problems. Research shows people spend more time planning their family vacation than planning how to make their earnings work in life.

We also think that earning more is a solution to overspending. It is NOT. The solution to overspending is to stop overspending. You can do this by making sure you aren't funding surface wants over true, deep needs.

We spend our precious time and energy earning money in order to use it for things we want and need in our lives. It is important to make sure our earnings are funding our highest values. I ask myself this question when I spend my earnings: "Is this worth the time I spent earning it?"

The answer to this question influences my spending choice. It can influence yours as well.

Words of Wisdom From Trusted Financial Planners About Earning and Investing

Rich Chambers

CFP®, Founder of Investor's Capital Management

"Find something you love and do that" is good advice as long as the doing makes enough to live on (including savings). When you are doing something you love, then it doesn't seem much like work and you'll gladly give it your all.

If you're not sure what you want to do, work with a Registered Life Planner (RLP®) to find out. While you're at it, try to love something that you can do as your own business. That way you get your "salary" and you get the "profit" from the business. If you work for someone else, you only get your salary, while the owners (shareholders) keep all the profit. There are also many tax advantages to having your own business.

The second part of earning is also important: you must invest your savings wisely. This sounds easy, and there is no end of advice about how to invest. But 95% of the advice is bad and is really meant to get you to invest in a way that provides an expensive benefit to someone other than you. So ignore most of the stuff you hear about investing.

Do spend some time learning how to invest wisely, however. I strongly recommend that you read John Bogle's book *Bogle on Mutual Funds*. And if you don't want to do the investing yourself, hire a trusted professional—someone who is your *fiduciary* (a fiduciary is a financial professional who places the client's interest above their own financial interest; ask them if they're your fiduciary 100% of the time). Eventually your savings and investments will produce more income than your earnings.

Sheryl Garrett
CFP®, AIF®, Founder of the Garrett Planning Network, Inc

Americans do not recognize or tend to take ownership of the fact we can have more income than we earn at our jobs. We can take on a second job, start a business, or do seasonal work to increase our earnings and do what it takes to save for the things we want to have and do in our lives. Finding ways to creatively earn money trumps using credit cards or an investment account as an income stream.

Make sure you are earning enough to fund your savings and investment accounts, so that your money outlives you, rather than you outliving your money.

Gifford Lehman
MBA, CFP®, Founder of Integris Wealth Management

A word about investing your earnings. I like to say that investing is one of those interesting conundrums—it is both far simpler and far more complex than you ever imagined. As an investment professional, I am well aware of the complexities. And while these complexities are important, they are only important AFTER the simple stuff has been attended to. This is what simple is:

- The biggest factor in your portfolio's return is your percentage of stocks versus bonds. This factor is the one you need to spend the most time on.

- The second biggest factor in portfolio performance is fees. Expensive investments are not expensive because they are better. They are just more expensive.

- The biggest factor in your portfolio's risk is a lack of diversification.

- The biggest factor in maintaining your diversification is disciplined rebalancing. Once a year is probably enough.

With just these four concepts, you will do better than 90% of all investors. However, most financial advice is about portfolio complexity, because that is what makes the advisor seem smart or expert—not because it's the most important.

Teresa Scagliotti
CFP®, Founder of Scagliotti and Associates Financial Planning

If you can, do what you love, as you will be in your earning years for a long time. If you can't work at what you love, know what your income really is and keep track of it. Take advantage of all sources of earning potential, particularly when it comes to employer benefits; while you might not see it in your checkbook, these will ultimately boost your bottom line.

Hilary Martin
MBA, CFP®, Healthy Wealthy Families

You come into this world with whatever resources you're born with. It's your job to find out what your special gifts and resources are and to share those with the world. Monetizing your internal gifts and innate talents can help you amass money. Financially, it's your job to amass enough savings that your dollars can work for you—through the beauty of compound interest—when you can no longer work for you or choose to no longer work. That is your financial empire, your wealth, your retirement savings; effectively cultivated, it will take good care of you.

Joanna Nowak

MBA, CFP®, Principal, MoneyWise Financial Advisors

A difficult economy separates hobbyists from serious entrepreneurs and professionals. So if you're serious about your craft, profession, calling—and you're able to confirm that what you have to offer is needed and adds value—then ask for what you're worth. Don't be afraid to look at increasing your earnings as an opportunity to create value, so that you get more of what you want and, in the process, offer solutions to clients' needs/problems/issues.

Ready, Set, EARN: Action Items To Put YOU Back in the Driver's Seat of Your Financial Future

What could you create today that would earn you $100? Yep, right now. What would that be for you? Here's the thing. This isn't about money. It's about you coming up with a creative idea that opens the door to money. Then it's about you putting legs on your idea and taking action steps to make it happen.

For me, if I wanted to earn $100 right now, here are the ideas that come to mind:

1. Let my neighbors know I'm open for dog walking. Our neighborhood is full of working people with pets.

2. Release some things I no longer use or need on eBay. I can think of about $3000 worth of stuff right now. Then I would see if any friends had stuff to sell and do it for them for a 40% cut.

3. Create a financial workshop for college students who are just now learning to go out on their own. I have contacts that could help me make this happen fast.

4. Create a class on Visioning and Imagination and offer it to my client list. That could fill in one week and bring in lots more than $100.

5. De-clutter a room for someone. I am really good at organizing and keeping life simple yet functional.

Okay, how about you? What are you willing to create to bring in $100? Write your ideas down in the space below:

1.

2.

3.

4.

5.

Now guess what? If you bring in $100 one time, you can bring in $100 repeatedly. You can become your own money-making machine!

Chapter 5

SAVINGS

Save a part of your income and begin now, for the man with a surplus controls circumstances and the man without a surplus is controlled by circumstances.

—Henry Buckley

"In the south, we have a saying: the poor save for Friday night and the rich save for the next generation," says my Wall Street journalist friend. This isn't because the rich are smarter than the poor; it's because the rich know the power of planning.

If you asked my mom, she'd tell you "saving money" has become a lost art, just like baking pies. Rarely do you go into a bank these days and actually see piggy banks to give out to kids. And kids, who are visual and concrete in their thinking, are losing any possibility of connectedness with money because it's becoming more of a concept—we can't touch the crispness of it, smell it, see it, or hear the jingle of change in our pockets. Money just isn't seen so much anymore; it moves through virtual transactions instead of being exchanged human hand to human hand.

Nor do we see television advertising encouraging the saving of money. In fact, it's just the opposite. We're more likely to be guided to images of refinancing or taking out a business loan.

Modern entrepreneurial magazines tout saving money as a "traditional" way to fund the future. A more modern approach is to earn money as the need or want arises throughout our life cycle, an "earn-as-you-go" approach.

My financial planner friend Tracy Lasecke tells me inherited wealth these days lasts only about three generations—unlike the inherited wealth of past generations of wealthy families like the Rockefellers, Kennedys, and Vanderbilts. The difference? The wealth of generations past was steeped in disciplined savings and investing strategies.

Unfortunately, as a culture, we are saving less and spending beyond our earnings. As reported in the *Huffington Post*, the Rasmussen Reports for Country Financial show that about 50 percent of the people surveyed do not set monthly savings goals, and half of Americans are spending more than they earn. We are upside down in our thinking and actions about what it takes to create a stable financial foundation. Creating adequate savings and investments is important to our overall financial health and well-being—but even though people understand this intellectually, behaviors that support a saving and investment mindset are lacking.

In fact, there are three BIG, IMPORTANT reasons to first SAVE and then INVEST money: staying out of debt, dodging life's curveballs, and caring for our "future selves." In this chapter we'll talk about all three, as well as how to build what I call a "successful saver mindset."

Reason #1: To Stay Out of Debt

Each of us needs to save money for expenses that come up over a given year outside our regular monthly expenses, IF we don't want to go into debt. I call these Seasonal Expenses.

Examples of Seasonal Expenses are: annual insurance premiums, property taxes, out-of-pocket medical, dental, vision costs, auto repairs/registration/maintenance, vacations, annual vet check-ups, holidays, summer camps for kids, and tuition, to name a few.

It sounds like common sense to save for these types of expenses so you don't go into credit card debt. Yet, until I learned about this concept, I didn't save for them. And these were the EXACT expenses that got placed on my credit card and—year after year—created a snowball effect of debt for me that quickly spun out of control. Not to mention the thousands of dollars I spent over time in high interest charges on this debt. This was money down the toilet.

If money isn't saved for these type of expenses, then one usually funds these expenses one of four ways: out of extra monthly cash flow, on a credit card, taking out a 401K loan to pay for accumulated expenses (that were initially placed on a credit card), or tapping into a home equity line of credit.

Here's what you can do to make sure you don't find yourself in one of these traps. I recommend opening a separate savings account earmarked for Seasonal Expenses. This is your first type of savings to fund fully before you fund the other two types of savings buckets (coming up). The mindset to have around this type of savings is this: what goes in will come out guilt free!

Here's how this first bucket of savings works. If these expenses are saved for each month, then when the expense arises, money is taken out of savings and transferred to checking to pay for the expense—and no debt is incurred. Psychologically, you will begin to create a healthy dependency on your savings to fund these expenses, rather than an unhealthy dependency on credit cards to fund these expenses.

Exercise

Make a list of all Seasonal Expenses that are likely to come up for you and your family over the next twelve months, with your best educated guess for the cost of each expense, in the quarter of the year that expense will most likely occur in. I will share my list with you to show you how it's done, then you can do your own.

Seasonal Expenses	Jan - March	April - June	July - Sept	Oct - Dec	Yearly Totals
Home Insurance			$900		$900
Auto Insurance			$1800		$1800
Umbrella Insurance			$300		$300
Auto Repairs	$500		$500	$500	$1500
Property Taxes		$3500		$3500	$7000
Vacation/Travel	$500	$5000	$500		$6000
Eye Glasses	$1000				$1000
Dental Work			$1500		$1500
Vet Visits	$250	$250	$250	$250	$1000
Totals	**$2250**	**$8750**	**$5750**	**$4250**	**$21,000**

You can see here that I need to come up with $21,000 in savings to be able to fund these expenses, if I don't want to go into debt. This means I'll need to make sure that each month I save money for these non-monthly expenses.

This type of savings needs to be funded BEFORE the other savings buckets, and here's why. If you don't fund this first, and instead you fund your retirement account (which is what I see in about 99 percent of my clients), then when these expenses occur, there will be a tendency to dip into your retirement account to fund these expenses. Not only will you pay taxes on the money taken out, but you'll also receive a penalty for dipping into your retirement account early.

Reason #2: To Dodge Life's Curveballs

If you are of a certain age, you know life throws curveballs. These curveballs come in the form of illness, death of a partner, job loss, and natural disasters, to name a few. Other expected curveballs are aging parents and life transitions.

I've found if I have money saved for the purpose of these curveballs, then my emotional energy stays focused on moving through what life places before me. I find I move through transitions more quickly when I can use my energy to process events, rather than directing my energy to survival thoughts such as, "How am I going to pay the mortgage?"

Saving money in a Safety Net account lets me rest my head on my pillow at night worry free. It gives me an experience of calm and freedom, knowing I'm covered for a period of time—enough time to allow myself to process my options, to problem solve, and to find a way to make life work again.

Sometimes, the innocent thinking of our youth or denial of our aging self becomes our obstacle to saving money for our Safety Net savings. But I believe the mindsets of "I don't need to save money because I'm going to work until I die" and "I'll earn money as I go in life to meet my needs and wants as they arise" are based in rationalization, denial, and wishful thinking.

These mindsets are a set-up for both failure and stress, because this thinking supports a lack of planning for the unexpected. And one of the best strategies in creating a solid financial foundation is planning for the unexpected. If the unexpected doesn't happen, we're home free. If it does, we're prepared.

Saving money for our short- and long-term needs is calming to our nervous system. Why? Because the security of a financial cushion is comforting and tells our nervous system we have enough for survival needs, plus some. Creating a cushion takes our nervous system out of the experience of living on the edge and not being prepared. This means less anxiety and fear. Even cavemen and cavewomen stored food for the winter months. This was their savings cushion so they would have enough when there were no animals to be found.

Exercise

Once you have funded your Seasonal Expense savings account, it's time to fund your Safety Net savings account. Here's how to get started. First, open a savings account just for your Safety Net savings and put in the minimum amount your bank requires to keep the account open.

Then, track your expenses for two to three months. Get clear on the range of money your monthly expenses cost you. Begin slowly. Make the decision to begin saving money to fund one month of your regular expenses in your Safety Net savings account. You might begin with putting $50 into this account each month. Then $100 and so on.

Once you've completed saving for one month of your regular expenses, save for another, then another. You can talk with your financial planner about the best savings vehicle for your Safety Net Savings Account. You won't earn much interest housing this money in a bank savings account, but the upside is it will be easy to access.

You might consider a Certificate of Deposit with a higher interest rate to house some of this money. Some CDs have early withdrawal penalties, while others do not. Your financial planner will know the best place to house your Safety Net Savings Account money.

Reason #3: To Care for Our Future Self

If we don't save and invest money for our future self's needs and wants, who will? Living to 100 years old or a little beyond is common today.

When I was in my forties, I had the mindset that I would work until I was seventy years of age with no problem. Unfortunately, at that point, I hadn't met my mid-fifties self. My life energy has changed—and so have my values. Time is now more important to me than money; I want to work less, not more. But my younger self didn't know this.

The very best time to begin saving for your future self is when you're in your early twenties and you have your first job. If your employer makes available to you the offerings of putting money away tax deferred, in a 401K, 403B, or an account of this nature, then take that opportunity. The earlier you begin to save for your retirement, the less painful saving money is, because your savings will grow beautifully with the magic of compounding interest over time. If you let your accounts grow (without taking money out), by the time you are in your sixth decade, you will have created a nice nest egg to support yourself in your later years.

And, if you're like me and depleted the money you had saved in your retirement accounts to fund lifestyle choices, then you'll have some catching up to do, just like me.

For those of us who are "late savers," we'll need to save more money in less time. If you're over fifty years of age, you can contribute $5000 dollars more to your 401K retirement account each year, on top of the regular maximum amount the government says you can contribute. For example, this year, everyone has the opportunity to contribute $17,500 to a 401K, and if you're over fifty years of age, you can contribute another $5000. These amounts change year to year based on what maximum contribution amounts our government sets for us.

If your employer doesn't offer a tax-deferred 401K retirement savings, you can still save for your later years by opening an IRA on your own and contributing the most you're allowed to each year, or if you're in business for yourself, you can open your own business 401K. A financial planner can help you determine just how much money you need to save in this particular investment bucket, in order to feel secure about your long-term financial future and help you choose which investment strategies are best for your particular situation.

One of the biggest obstacles I see people face when it comes to saving for retirement is that current life challenges get funded first, and saving for retirement is consistently placed on the back burner. Being a parent of soon-to-be-college-age children is an example of this. Many parents feel guilty contributing to their retirement over fully funding their children's college education. Oftentimes, there is money to fund one of these areas but not both.

I frequently hear, "We made a promise to ourselves to pay our kids' college tuition, and that comes before our retirement savings." In this situation, I often remind parents of two things. First, their children are younger than they are, and their children have age on their side, giving them more time to pay off their own education. Second, not fully funding one's retirement fund sets up the potential in later years for dependency on the children, and no parent (or child) really wants to experience this role reversal.

Exercise

The first step in caring for your future self is to open a tax-deferred savings account, such as a 401K or an IRA. You can do this through your employer if an account of this nature is offered, or, if you are self-employed, you can open up your own 401K or IRA. If you're opening a retirement account on your own, consult with your financial planner as to which type is best for you.

Building Your Successful Saver Mindset

Common wisdom says that once you receive your earnings, the first person to pay is yourself. It's also common wisdom that smoking is bad for your health—but just because we know something to be true doesn't mean we align our behavior with it.

Being successful at saving money has in part to do with a mindset that thinks beyond the here and now (or Friday night). This mindset values one's future self. It both understands and is moved by a deeper wisdom that our younger self may not fully know in terms of what lies ahead for our older self. It saves for life's curveballs.

Successful savers pay themselves first and live off of what is left over. The flow of money goes like this: Earn, Save, Spend rather than Earn, Spend, Save.

I bet you're thinking, "Well, what if I already have the habit in place of spending before saving?" You aren't alone; I used to spend before saving money too. It takes time to practice paying oneself first. Start small. Celebrate baby steps. Even depositing money into one of your savings or investment accounts first, BEFORE you pay your other bills, is a way of honoring the flow of EARN, SAVE, and SPEND.

Find ways to lower your lifestyle ceiling and divert money to savings. Let me give you an example. I come from a line of women who have decorative dishes to celebrate each holiday, along with decorations, table linens, and other specialty items. When I was in the space of examining my expenses in order to look at ways I could cut costs in order to save more money, I was drawn to look at all the stuff in my kitchen.

All my stuff not only overwhelmed me, I had run out of cupboard space to store it all! I made a decision to let go of ALL the specialty items. I sold much of it on eBay and some at consignment stores. I then bought white dishes, classy and appropriate for every occasion, and now use colored napkins or flowers from my garden to make an event special. I no longer spend money on household items for decoration. This saves me lots of money each year.

Another example of lowering my lifestyle ceiling was letting go of my gym membership, which I paid monthly. I enjoyed going to the gym, but I wasn't one of the regulars. I decided to stop my membership and made a commitment to myself to hike hills, enjoy nature, and sweat with my girlfriends. I'm now on my eleventh year of hiking, and I love it. This was a savings of about $200 a month, which I now place in my savings account.

Each time you get a raise at work or give yourself a raise, if you're in business for yourself, bank that money instead of increasing your lifestyle expenses. Make that money count. Successful savers keep lifestyle choices flat (the same amount) and place increased incremental earnings toward savings and investment accounts. They get that a little here and a little there adds up to big money over time.

Successful savers set good boundaries and say *no* to expenses that take them off their plan. For example, last year my husband and I wanted to do some remodeling on our home. We created a budget and saw that if we chose to do the remodeling on our home, we couldn't do much else, like a vacation. Of course, we wanted both.

We were proud of ourselves that we decided to do the remodeling and not the vacation. Instead, we planned lots of fun, inexpensive day trips with our dogs in the San Francisco Bay area. We hiked some amazing trails that were new to us. We actually had more fun with all the little things we did in being creative than taking a vacation for two weeks.

Save through automated systems. What you don't see you won't spend. Otherwise, our minds tend to fantasize about what we want to buy next, when we see we have a surplus of money hanging out in our checking accounts.

Successful savers find saving money pleasurable and enjoy witnessing the growth of their money over time (I very much look forward to receiving my Schwab statements each month to see how my retirement accounts have grown). They also live within their means and don't accrue revolving credit-card debt.

Working with a financial planner helps you build your savings muscle. When you create your long-term financial plan, you will begin to stretch your thinking to what is needed beyond the here and now. Each year I meet with my financial planner and advisor to make sure I'm on target for saving for my future. It's one of the best things I do for myself each year. I liken it to the annual physical I schedule with my medical doctor to make sure my physical health is in order.

You can become a successful saver, regardless of your age or past history—it's a learned behavior. One of my best successful savings stories is a client I'll call Tammy. Tammy entered my office a chronic overspender and very high earner with no savings at all. She liked to spend money on clothes that hung in her closet with price tags attached. She had to work hard to overcome her overspending.

One of our appointments together landed on her birthday. She came into my office crying. I was worried that something was wrong, but when I asked her why she was crying, she said, "I'm so happy. I have $500 in my savings, and I've never even had a savings before. I received a lot of presents today, even a dozen long-stemmed red roses from my boyfriend. Nothing, nothing compares to the feeling of gratitude I have today of having money in my savings."

Words of Wisdom From Trusted Financial Advisors About Saving Money

Rich Chambers

CFP®, Founder of Investor's Capital Management

The best financial advice I ever received was quite simple. When I was in the Air Force, the officer's club would bring people in to speak to us. Once a mutual fund group talked mostly about how we could use their mutual funds, but one of them also said, "Pay yourself first." The advice was to save 10% of your gross pay.

So I started doing that and never stopped. Today, with lower expected value of Social Security payments, I recommend to young clients that they save 15% of their gross. This can include 401(K) contributions, even the amounts the employer contributes. What clients don't realize is that in doing so, they accomplish two things: the obvious, saving, and the less obvious, spending less.

Sheryl Garrett

CFP®, AIF®, Founder of the Garrett Planning Network, Inc.

I assume Americans spend 100 percent of what they bring home in pay, which is why savings must be automatic and taken out of one's paycheck before take-home money hits the checking account. When you don't see it, you don't miss it.

A penny saved is NOT a penny earned. A penny saved is MORE THAN a penny earned, when placed in the market with the magic of compound interest. That said, many people think returns on their nest egg alone will solve their problem of not having enough saved for their later years. Not so. The stock market's rate of return can't bail people out or be a rescue strategy for folks who don't save consistently, over time, with persistence until they retire.

Condition yourself to save more over time, just like you would gradually increase any good habit over time, like exercising. When you increase contributions to your 401K by one to two percent, then adjust your lifestyle to your new savings rate. Then increase your savings rate again and readjust your lifestyle again. Keep doing this while working with your financial planner until you are meeting your long-term investment goals. Slow, steady, and sure is the way to go.

Remember the common wisdom phrase, save 10% of your income? You need to understand that saving 10% works if you begin saving at twenty-five years old and retire at sixty-five years old. If you start saving at 40 years old, that percentage triples.

Save little bits as early as possible and always pay yourself first. Pay down debt. Keep your focus on ways you can increase your net worth. You will meet your goals if you stay focused and practice behaviors that increase your net worth.

Gifford Lehman

MBA, CFP®, Founder of Integris Wealth Management

Pay yourself first. In all my years as a financial planner, this is probably the biggest determinant of someone's financial success. Notice that I did not say that how much money you make is the most important variable in one's financial success. If you earn $1 million a year and spend $1.5 million per year, you will be a financial failure, along with all the emotional angst and drama that goes with that.

This was well said by Charles Dickens in his book *David Copperfield*. The line is: "Annual income twenty pounds, annual expenditure nineteen six, result happiness. Annual income twenty pounds, annual expenditure twenty pounds ought six, result misery."

The inability to "pay yourself first" is all about the psychology of money. It is about immediate gratification versus delayed gratification. It is about succumbing to the onslaught of consumerism in our society. There can be a huge personal payoff by taking the time to figure out what your values are and then behaving accordingly.

A story: Some middle-aged friends got married. It was the second marriage for the wife, who had a ten-year-old daughter. They were financially responsible and had no debt except for their mortgage, but they had no savings.

As a wedding present I gave them six months of financial planning. They each had earnings of about $40,000 for a total of about $80,000. A key planning message was that if they ever wanted to retire without becoming dependent upon their daughter or society, they needed to start saving.

They said it was impossible. There was nothing to cut. This was because they were thinking in terms of paying themselves last.

A few years later, they decided it was important to homeschool their daughter. This meant that the wife cut back her work to the point that she was only making $10,000 per year. The husband worked harder and increased his earnings to $50,000. What was interesting is that they were not stressed about the net loss of $20,000 in earnings.

Seemingly with no pain, they made adjustments to their spending.

The message here, and a key element of paying yourself first, is that it is human nature to spend whatever you have. And if you pay yourself first, then whatever is left is what you will spend.

(There is a small book called *The Richest Man in Babylon* that makes this point better than I could. The book is a collection of stories, and this particular story of the same name is about five pages. I recommend you read the story, which you can find at www.ccsales.com/the_richest_man_in_babylon.pdf.)

Teresa Scagliotti
CFP®, Founder of Scagliotti and Associates Financial Planning

Get in the habit early in life of paying yourself first—if you don't see it, you won't spend it! Make sure you fund all categories of savings: emergency, retirement, other goals (new car, new home, vacation). Even the smallest amount of savings is helpful.

As for how best to invest these funds, your timeline will be important, as well as your tolerance for risk. Monies that are near-term and for an emergency need to be liquid and readily available. The same might be true for goals as well, depending on the goal. Retirement savings are long-term, and, as a result, there is the potential for growth over the long term in the market.

The only guarantee you have is that the market will go up and go down. Know what type of investor you are. Do you want to do it yourself? Do you want to have an advisor? Either way, the allocation of your investments needs to be based on your retirement goal.

If you know when you're going to retire, and you know what your expenses and retirement income are (think pension, social security), then you'll know the amount of money you need to have in the pot when you retire; this will also tell you the rate of return you need to achieve that goal. Chasing the highest returns most likely will not get you to your goal.

Hilary Martin
MBA, CFP®, Healthy Wealthy Families

The truth that doesn't often come out in the mainstream media is that, at this point, investing is really a science that shouldn't involve any guessing or reacting. Investing is an activity in which unlimited returns and unlimited wealth are potentially available (keyword: potentially), and some of the smartest minds in the world have been hard at work for years trying to crack the code. And it's done—the heavy lifting is done, and we know how to invest and maximize the chances that you'll earn what the market will reliably pay you.

You have to suffer the downs to enjoy the ups, and all of the evidence we have says that most investors need a behavior coach to keep them invested during the downs. As an individual investor, please don't go it alone. Find an advisor you trust, one who tells a story similar to the one I've told here, who doesn't try to sell you annuities or individual stocks or products they earn a commission on. Find an advisor who knows the science of investing and let them help you. I like to say that your investing should be boring—so that the life it enables can be exciting.

Ready, Set, SAVE: Action Items to Put YOU Back in the Driver's Seat of Your Financial Future

1. What is your next step toward saving money? What savings bucket is YOUR next bucket to fund? Seasonal Expenses? Dodging Life's Curveballs Account? Saving for Your Future-Self Account?

2. When will you take action?

3. What will you reward yourself with for taking action—
   that doesn't cost any money?

Chapter 6

SPENDING

We can tell our values by looking at our checkbook stubs.
—Gloria Steinem

When you think of planning your spending before you spend, do you think "restriction" or "freedom?" If you think "restriction," you're in the majority! Many of my clients tell me, "If I plan my spending, it will mean I won't be able to buy what I want."

What if planning your spending actually helped you get more of what you wanted? What if planning your spending helped you to work less and to be able to spend more time with your family? What if planning your spending helped you to prioritize and fund what was most important to you, giving you an experience of internal fulfillment?

What if planning your spending helped you to know with confidence you were creating a financial future that could support you when you no longer wanted to work for a living? And what if planning your spending would allow you to avoid the fear of being dependent on your children or society?

Our minds play tricks on us by telling us if we plan, we won't get what we want. But if we plan our spending, we actually get *more* of what we want, because we get to make conscious choices about where and how we spend our money. When we don't plan our spending, money leaks and travels into areas that don't always give us true value for what we just spent it on.

In this chapter we'll talk about tracking your money as a way to get a handle on your income/expense ration, the methods we use to spend money (cash, credit, etc.), how each method influences our spending habits, and traps that increase our spending ceiling without our realizing it. We'll also talk about the neuroscience of spending, and we'll finish by helping you get started tracking your own spending.

Tracking

The best way to begin consciously knowing where your money goes is to start tracking your expenses. Tracking is the first step in bringing us into a more conscious connection with our money, making the shift from living in financial vagueness to a space of financial clarity. Tracking visually allows us to see *where* money is going, as well as how much is going out.

When I first started tracking, I was surprised at how many times a month I found myself in stores that sold candles and soap. I was even more surprised at how much I spent. I didn't really need more candles and lavender soap; I already had a significant stash of both, an entire large bathroom drawer full.

What I learned from tracking my money was that I went shopping to indulge my olfactory senses, to take a break from the busyness of life, to give myself the pleasure of a distraction. By going olfactory shopping, I was engaging in the need to have a little more leisure in my day. When I recognized my true need, I was able to give myself other options that were kinder to my bank account, like taking a walk in nature and enjoying natural fragrances.

Through tracking, my husband found that he liked to hang out at Home Depot and buy energy-saving lightbulbs and gadgets.

He wanted to make sure our home—his cave—was adequately supplied. So we had an entire drawer of energy-saving light bulbs in our garage, enough to last for quite a while! He too began to see how he spent blindly.

A little spending here and a little spending there can add up to significant dollars going out in a month's time. Tracking our money really helped us to see the expense blind spots we were living in. This awareness then helped us to make better spending choices that were more in alignment and integrity with our shorter- and longer-term goals.

We've been tracking our money since 1992, and one of the blessings from this experience is that we have problem-solved our way through unexpected life transitions with grace and ease, because we knew how much we were spending and what we were spending on. We could adjust those expense numbers with confidence by putting behaviors behind them that lowered our lifestyle ceiling when we needed to.

For example, when we were dealing with a job transition in our family, my husband found ways to cut our grocery costs, while still managing to buy high-quality food. We went from shopping weekly at higher-end grocery stores for meat and produce to purchasing our meat at Costco and buying produce at our local farmer's market. We saved five hundred dollars a month just with this behavioral change.

And the big bonus here was that when the job transition period was over, we stayed at our new lifestyle ceiling with food costs and banked the five hundred dollars a month we had saved during the job transition, instead of going back to spending more on food.

My clients are frequently surprised, when they begin tracking, to find automatic expenses being taken out of their checking accounts for services they no longer use. Sometimes we find we pay for service plans that we don't fully use, when a service plan of a lesser cost will be more kind to our cash flow. Tracking helps us to evaluate the worthiness of an expense.

Some questions I ask myself are: "Is this expense worth the time it took me to earn the money required to purchase this?" "What need am I trying to meet by funding this expense?" "Does this expense move me closer or take me further away from my financial goals?"

Besides helping us to shine light on our spending blind spots, tracking can shine light on the gap between income and planned expenses. This information alone is huge. When expenses exceed income, the opportunity at hand is to realign with our highest life priorities, which support us in making decisions to help us live within our means.

Spending with Cash, Credit, Check, or ATM Debit Card

When I ask clients why they use credit cards, I primarily hear a version of one of two reasons: "Because I'm not sure of the amount of money in my bank account, and I don't want to be embarrassed at a checkout counter if my ATM debit card doesn't go through." Or "I earn airline miles for each purchase I make."

One of the reasons I advocate the use of an ATM debit card or cash for purchases is, obviously, that there is a direct correlation between what is spent and the amount of money left in one's wallet or bank account. Using payment options that keep us connected and conscious to our money helps us to stay in power around our choices and to make decisions based on our spending priorities.

Research shows that when a credit card is used to pay for an item or service, there is a tendency for us to spend more, sometimes 20 to 30 percent more than we would if we were using a payment option that had a direct effect on our bank account. Often, credit cards give us the illusion that we have more to spend than we actually do. It's easy to think, "Oh, I'll put it on the card," rather than think, "Hmmm ... what effect will this have on my bank account, and what other expenses will I need to adjust downward in order to make this expense fit into my cash-flow plan?"

Some of my clients do use credit cards wisely and prefer using one credit card for all spending over a given month instead of cash or an ATM debit card. In this situation, however, clients use pristine behaviors. They first plan all their expenses on their monthly spending plan, and, second, they make sure planned income exceeds planned expenses for any given month. Then, they only place planned expenses on their credit card and pay the card off in full, in the same month the expenses were incurred. This way they earn airline miles without earning interest on any revolving credit-card debt.

It's an interesting phenomenon that money is becoming more of a concept in our modern world and less a concrete thing. We hardly touch, see, or hear the crinkling of a crisp dollar bill or the jingle of change anymore. I remember loving the smell of a new dollar bill when I was growing up! As a society we are becoming less and less connected with our money—namely because we are no longer bringing a sensory experience to this part of our lives.

While digital transactions are convenient and modern, they offer less engagement and less connection, making it more difficult to know what our true financial picture is at any given moment.

Traps That Increase Our Spending Ceiling

1. Comparing Ourselves to Others

When we compare ourselves with others, like our friends and neighbors, and compare the stuff and experience they have to what we have, we enter dangerous waters. Comparing with others creates a mindset of lack in our lives. Someone has something and someone doesn't. Our focus is usually on what we don't have.

A way to escape the comparison mindset is to practice gratitude. Be grateful for what you have in your life, especially all the stuff money can't buy. Grateful people spend less because their focus isn't on "having more"; their focus is on "being thankful for what is." These two mindsets cannot co-exist at the same time.

2. The Scarcity Mindset

The "I-have-to-have-it-now-because-it-won't-be-there-tomorrow" thinking is a trap that increases our spending ceiling. This is usually a rationalization to justify the urgency of an expense. It can also be a pattern of immediate gratification linked to poor impulse control. I recommend that, when an urgency arises and there's a feeling of "have to have," a person go home, think about the thing they want to purchase, and, if the intensity of the desire remains three days later, then re-evaluate the expense and look at what need it's really satisfying.

In twelve-step groups there is an acronym, HALT. Each letter represents a word of warning about negative emotional states: Hungry, Angry, Lonely, or Tired. If you're hungry, angry, lonely, or tired, it's best not to go shopping. Negative feeling states predispose you to spend more, because spending can be a temporary mood elevator. If you're in a negative feeling state, stay home from the shopping malls or surfing the internet to make purchases. Instead, find another way to soothe your nervous system and to support yourself to a more positive state of being.

3. Overspending

Spending beyond our planned spending or what our income allows can make us at times feel like a failure, out of control, and put us in a place of self-loathing. When this happens, we might think, "What's the use, I've already spent over my planned spending, so why not spend more and get these extras?" Spending beyond my plan happens at times for me too. That doesn't mean we *have* to spend more. We can stop where we are, re-calibrate, and embrace the concept of "do no more harm spending" from this place forward.

If we have given ourselves the identity of an overspender, we need to be willing to shed that identity for the sake of our financial future and to practice behaviors of balanced earning and spending. Balance will bring control back to our lives and ground us.

4. Life Stressors

Life stressors, such as loss, life transitions, marital problems, someone cutting us off on a freeway, a new baby, sleep deprivation, and stress at work can get us to go shopping. But rather than going shopping to distract us from life stressors, we can find other ways to manage stress, which in the long run is kinder to our bank accounts, as well as our body, mind, and spirit. Some ideas could be to take a hot shower or bath, exercise, watch a funny movie, get a massage, or talk your stress out with a person you trust.

5. Sudden Wealth

Sometimes high earnings, sudden or inherited wealth, or winning the lottery can expand our spending ceiling. When we have more money than we are accustomed to having, subconsciously we can "spend down" the money until we get back to the comfort zone of what we can easily manage. It's common knowledge that many lottery winners lose their winnings within a five-year period. Some suggest it's because a large amount of money can be overwhelming, and people that come into sudden wealth aren't used to managing large sums of money.

Howard, one of my sudden-wealth clients was in the process of getting married. Two weeks before he was to wed his bride, she died in a car accident. Unbeknownst to Howard, she had left him three million dollars in a stock portfolio.

Deeply saddened by his loss, Howard didn't want the money. He felt survivor guilt and said to me, "How can I spend this money and receive joy from it when I will be reminded with each cent I spend of the loss of my fiancé?" He wanted to donate the entire three million to charity, just to get the money out of his orbit. It felt "dirty" to him.

His financial planner and I worked with him and asked him to consider waiting one year before taking any action on the inherited money, which he agreed to do.

During that year, his grieving process shifted his perspective. Instead of feeling guilty about receiving the money, he was able to shift to the reality that this money was a symbol of his fiancé's love. Deep gratitude replaced guilt, and he used the money to fund his highest dreams and passion: purchasing a farm in Northern California and growing organic vegetables.

6. Mental Illness

Another trap that can increase our spending ceiling is when mental health issues are present, in the form of depression, substance dependence, or mania in bipolar illness. Because spending can elevate mood, many people that suffer from these disorders overspend. The grandiosity that can be present in mania, where people want to be noticed or to receive praise from others, can even elicit a spending spree.

Prednisone, an anti-inflammatory steroid, can also create a state of mania. I've had clients come to me who've said, "I went out and bought all new furniture for my home when I was on Prednisone." They call it steroid furniture.

The Neuroscience of Spending Money

A few years ago, Carnegie Mellon University did a study on the neural predictors of purchasing. George Lowenstein, professor of economics and psychology at Carnegie Mellon, along with Brian Knutson from Stanford University and Drazen Prelec from the Massachusetts Institute of Technology, studied how people make purchasing decisions.

These scientists looked into people's brains, using a neuro-imaging machine that measured blood flow to certain regions of the brain while showing people pictures of items they could purchase, along with the cost of the item. The researchers knew by observing where blood flowed in the brain if a person would say yes or no to a purchase most of the time.

This study suggests that different parts of the brain work in the various stages of making a purchasing decision to buy or not to buy. In fact, three parts of the brain are involved with a purchasing decision: the *nucleus accumbens* and the *insula*, which live in the midbrain, and the *prefrontal cortex*, which lives in the forebrain.

The nucleus accumbens is the pleasure center of the brain, rich in dopamine receptors. When dopamine is released, we feel happy—and this part of the brain associates "having" with "happiness." But it cares only about pleasure, not consequences. In the study, when consumers liked a potential purchase, the nucleus accumbens lit up like a Christmas tree because of the happy, free-floating dopamine.

When the price of the potential purchase was introduced, and the consumer thought the price to be more than the value received from the purchase, the insula—also known as the "tightwad" of the brain—lit up. In this case the consumer was most likely to make the decision not to purchase the item shown to them in the neuroimaging scan.

If the consumer felt the price of the purchase was a good deal and with proportionate value, the frontal cortex did the number crunching, thought out the consequences that came with the expense, and said yes to the purchase.

Why is this preliminary research important? It may begin to give us clues about how and why we make spending decisions. This research also has practical application in the real world of spending. Think about it: what needs to happen in order for the insula (the tight-wad) to let down its guard so the consumer can more easily say yes to a purchase?

For example, shopping at stores like Costco lowers the insula's price/value ratio and makes it easier for the consumer to spend money. Our insula knows that Costco gives us the best deals and value. That's why all of us can go into Costco with a list of five items and come out with an overloaded buggy. Credit cards delay the purchasing pain of the insula as well. The buy-now-pay-later strategy tricks the insula into delayed pain.

On the other hand, financial consultants like myself encourage clients to spend with cash or an ATM debit card, because this activates the insula and can slow down spending—important because pain is associated with a decreasing balance in one's checking account with each expense incurred.

Words of Wisdom From Trusted Financial Advisors About Spending Money

Rich Chambers
CFP®, Founder of Investor's Capital Management

Don't buy a horse or a boat. Do buy a home when you can afford to pay at least 20 percent down and you expect to live there at least five years. Buy used cars unless a used car (adjusted for mileage) costs the same as a new car. Use good debt—home mortgage, investments in your business. Avoid bad debt—paying interest for anything that depreciates.

ALWAYS pay your credit cards off each month. Look for a credit card that pays you back in cash. Pay off loans with the highest interest rates first. Get a home equity line to use for emergencies, and then hope you never use it.

Sheryl Garrett
CFP®, AIF®, Founder of the Garrett Planning Network, Inc.

Never go to a shopping mall for exercise or entertainment. Go for a specific reason, with a list. If you do go to a shopping mall for exercise or entertainment, don't take money with you. Don't watch shopping channels on TV.

Create clear goals with savings targets for those goals. This gives you direction and motivation, and it becomes easier to stick to a spending plan. Track your spending, stay conscious. When you spend, ask yourself, "Does this decision affect my net worth?" If a particular spending decision does affect your net worth, pause … stop, look, listen to what you're doing, take a cooling-off period, and come back to your decision to spend after a re-evaluation.

Use the TV program *Survivor* as your backdrop when thinking of Needs, Nice to Haves, and Luxury Items in your life. Ask yourself, what would be a Need for the people on that show? The answer would be water, fire, food, and shelter. Then ask what would be a Nice to Have for the people on *Survivor*? And a Luxury Item? Apply this thinking to your own lifestyle choices.

Teresa Scagliotti
CFP®, Founder of Scagliotti and Associates Financial Planning

Knowing how much you spend on a monthly and annual basis is incredibly important—it's the cornerstone of ALL financial planning. If we don't know how much we spend, we can't begin to plan for future goals.

Spending tells a story about a person—what's important to them, what they're passionate about, and if they're in troubled waters. We live in an economy today where you just don't get to see your money any longer. We're so removed from what we spend that we don't really know what we need. How do we know what we need as income if we don't know what we spend? Think tracking or monitoring of what you spend. There are many easy ways to accomplish this.

Hilary Martin
MBA, CFP®, Healthy Wealthy Families

For me, spending will probably always be lumpy. I'm a natural overspender, but I've managed to keep bad habits at bay for many years now. I have systems of bank accounts to keep money separate, and just one checking account from which I am allowed to spend money on things like food, clothes, entertainment, and gifts. Each time I get paid, some money gets transferred into that account. It isn't very much money; I make it a game to live well within my means. I admonish myself to make the money last, but the truth is I never do, and it actually completely works for me!

I love spending my money, and there are always things I want to do with it. The critical piece is that once I've spent most of what's in that checking account, I can't transfer more money in or spend from another account. I end up living darn frugally for the week before my next bi-monthly paycheck. The key is that I have a very empowering context for this process.

We tend to relate to overspenders as if they're irresponsible or that it's a shameful habit, and you've got to free yourself of that thought altogether. Know thyself, create a system, and then don't *ever* let guilt give you permission to reach into those other accounts! You could enact this system using a rewards credit card, as well—you'd just have to be absolutely vigilant about making sure the balance never gets up above your checking account balance, and then pay it off twice a month.

Joanna Nowak
MBA, CFP®, Principal, MoneyWise Financial Advisors

Deciding what to spend on is relatively easy once you are very clear about your goals in life, your dreams, and your aspirations. Once you have that clarity, you'll not want to spend on things/ experiences that don't support those goals; you'll save to reach those goals without feeling deprived. As an advisor I'd recommend you spend lavishly on that which is most important and cut spending mercilessly on what doesn't support your vision of your future.

Ready, Set, SPEND: Action Items to Put YOU Back in the Driver's Seat of Your Financial Future

For one month, track all of your expenses and income. Notice "ah-hah" moments, when you have new insight into areas you're spending money that don't provide you with that much value. Decide if you will continue to spend money in these areas or if you will divert this spending toward a longer-term financial goal, like your retirement savings or to pay off current credit card debt.

Remember, little bits of money from here and little bits of money from there add up to big bits of money!

Once you've tracked your expenses and income for one month, begin planning your spending. Sit down at the beginning of each month and plan where you're going to allocate the dollars that are available for spending in a given month. Compare your planned expenses with the amount of income you will receive in that same month. If expenses exceed income, go back and see what you can adjust down in expenses or ways you can bring more income in. Narrow the income/expense gap as much as you can.

This process can often move forward faster if you work with a financial coach. Sometimes we aren't able to see the perspective someone outside our situation can see, and two brains are always better than one when it comes to problem solving.

Chapter 7

GIVING

It's not how much we give but how much love we put into giving."

—*Mother Teresa*

The act of giving opens our hearts, minds, and spirits and is a behavior that says, "I have enough and I want you to have enough as well." Acts of generosity can take on many forms, but the act itself comes from a place of abundance deep down, without strings attached.

My mom and dad taught me how to give. When friends and family came to our home, they always went home with full bellies. My mom would begin a conversation at the kitchen table, and soon to follow would be an invitation to a fresh berry pie and coffee. My dad would add to this by going out to his half-acre garden in the summer and sending visitors home with offerings from its bounty; in the winter he'd send them home with canned or frozen goods from the summer garden.

When I was in grade school, I remember a neighbor's house burning to the ground. My dad gave offerings of food and some cash to our neighbor, then went above and beyond, going to the church we belonged to and asking the priest if the church could please give help to our neighbor until their homeowner's insurance kicked in. When the priest told my dad there was no help to be given because the neighbors "weren't part of our parish," my dad stopped going to that church for a long time.

Maybe it was growing up in a close-knit farming community, but early on, I got the sense we were all connected and it was our duty to make sure those around us had sufficiency in the way of survival needs. When a neighbor needed help, the community pitched in and gave it, and no money was exchanged. What was exchanged was a deep sense of gratitude, a hug, and sometimes a slap on the back.

This giving circle in the community I grew up in still goes on today. It helped me to see that giving is more about what comes from the heart than the pocketbook.

Rules of Healthy Giving

Healthy giving is good for the giver and receiver, both emotionally and financially. This means the giver isn't creating a deficit when giving, such as going into credit card debt, tapping into home equity lines of credit, taking out personal loans, or sacrificing the savings and investment part of their financial plan. It also means that the giving involved isn't hurting the receiver, enabling or rescuing him or her in some way that is harmful to their development as a human being.

One of the most common struggles I hear from my couple clients with children around giving has to do with funding their children's college education over their own retirement needs, which we talked about earlier. Although parenting is a role that involves a certain amount of self-sacrifice and placing the needs of our children as a high priority, it is important for parents to maintain their own financial foundation while giving to their children.

It reminds me of the standard "put on your own oxygen mask first," which we all hear from flight attendants when flying. Otherwise, parents set themselves up for vulnerability at a stage in life when finances are needed for their own survival needs.

I often have heart-to-heart conversations with couples who want to give to their children by paying in full for their college education, while depleting their retirement savings to do so. This isn't healthy giving, because it's hurting the giver and setting up a situation where the giver is not going to be financially taken care of in older age. While every parent wants the best for their children, it's important to look at BOTH the emotional and financial consequences of giving, both in the here and now and in the future.

Remember what was said in the savings chapter: when it comes to earning power, as well as time to pay off potential school debts, children have the gift of time on their side, while their parents do not. Of course, if parents can fully fund their own retirement accounts *and* give fully to their child's college education, that is another story.

Healthy giving is free of guilt or pressure to give more than one can monetarily afford to give. I've struggled with this rule of healthy giving myself, especially when my husband and I were in a time of transition and it was around the December holidays. He was in the middle of a job transition, and the holidays were almost upon us. Each month we were dipping into our "emergency savings" to make ends meet. While we had saved money just for a time like this, it didn't seem prudent for us to spend this emergency money on holiday gifts for ourselves or on those we loved—we didn't know how long he would be out of work.

We had all kinds of mind chatter going on in our heads: *Will family think we're cheap if we exclude ourselves from gift giving this year? Will we be judged? What will our friends think if we don't do a gift exchange?*

We decided to have a conversation with each of our families a couple of months prior to the holiday to let them know we wouldn't be partaking in a gift exchange that year.

To our surprise, both families had been thinking the same thing. My mom told me that she and my dad had everything they needed and wanted. She also said, "I think we should drop doing birthday gifts as well and just call each other and send wishes of love to one another on our birthdays." My husband's family expressed the same sentiment.

That year, we didn't even decorate or put up a tree. And the experience was one of true freedom. We broke free of the expectation of long-standing tradition and let go of the initial guilt we felt for breaking family gift-giving rules. In breaking tradition, this experience helped us reset in a creative way what we would do for holidays in the future.

Healthy giving has no expectations or strings attached. When we give to get, that is not healthy giving. Giving to get is a form of co-dependent giving and can be perceived as a form of manipulation, control, or power. I've witnessed many parents and their adult children in a "giving-to-get" dynamic.

The Spirit of Giving is pure when giving comes from loving kindness and we give out of joy, without expecting to receive any recognition back.

I've made a list here of some gifts from the heart that don't cost money and are, therefore, kind to your bank account. This is a place for you to begin to give and to practice the true Spirit of Giving—giving from the heart:

- Acceptance of another

- Acknowledgement of a kind act

- Encouragement when someone is down in the dumps

- Sharing gifts of the spirit—smiles, hugs, and laughter—to brighten someone's day

- Prayers of healing, protection, and blessings

- Giving a listening ear, as well as time to listen

- Writing a letter the old-fashioned way, with pen, paper, and a postage stamp

- Giving thanks for acts of kindness, thoughtfulness, and generosity

- Giving can take on many forms, which include giving of our time, energy, and resources, which includes money. But we are most emotionally free when we give from our hearts *and* from what our bank accounts can afford.

Thoughts on Tithing

The principle behind tithing is to give 10 percent of earnings to God before spending, saving, or giving money to other places. The idea is to then live off the money that is left, making life work financially without going into credit card debt.

In my financial consulting practice, I frequently come across this scenario: a hard-working, spiritual couple tithes while going deeper and deeper into credit card debt. While I honor the principle of tithing, I also honor the principle of financial well-being, and I don't view the stress created by increasing debt as well-being. I would suggest getting debt paid off first, and then, as debt is paid off, tithing can be reinstituted.

I realize many readers may disagree with this. I've even had religious leaders of a congregation tell my clients to continue to tithe while digging deeper and deeper holes of credit-card debt. I disagree with this approach, but I realize it's really up to you to follow your beliefs in deciding how to make tithing work in your life.

I also believe it's up to each of us to determine how much we give and when we give. A young couple starting out with a growing family may have increased expenses due to more mouths to feed, diapers to buy, and other expenses associated with new babies. So some life stages may open us to being able to give more with our resources than others.

Ethical Wills

Most of us are familiar with the purpose of a Living Will and Trust, which communicates how financial or material treasures are to be passed on to the living after our death. But what if you don't have a big inheritance to pass on to your kids? Or what if you want to make sure you gift your children or grandchildren a treasure more important than money?

There is a wonderful custom, a process that creates the passing on of legacy from one generation to another through written letter, to children or grandchildren. This process is called an Ethical Will, which communicates the treasures of your heart, not just the treasures in your investment accounts.

This tradition believes the wisdom acquired during a lifetime is just as valuable as the monetary wealth acquired during that same lifetime. Unlike a Living Will and Trust, Ethical Wills are not legally binding documents. They can come in a variety of forms, from a short one-page letter to a lengthy autobiographical statement to a bound album.

Creating an Ethical Will is a way to express deep-felt thoughts, feelings, hopes, life lessons, and personal and spiritual values to loved ones. It's a way to share the riches of your life experiences, a way to express what you desire for your children's lives, so that your values and lessons may live on in generations to come. As my direct-speaking, hometown estate attorney would say, "It's a way to still reach out and touch your children from your grave."

My grandmother Nellie created a form of Ethical Will prior to her death. She had twelve children, and while in her hospital bed, she summoned each of her children and their families, scheduling them to visit her at varying times over several days. During these visits she laid out instructions about how she wished them to lead their lives, reminded them to remember the values they had grown up with, and reiterated the "Golden Rule" to each family.

Her instructions remained powerful long after her passing. I remember when family disagreements would come up, my uncles would say, "Well, what would Mom want us to do?" I witnessed them behaving according to her instructions, rather than giving into more primitive ways of being.

Some people choose to share their Ethical Wills during life, usually at an important anniversary, family milestone, or other of life's major transitions. Some women with critical illness, such as cancer, have formed writing groups in order to hand down to their children their life messages.

Passing on your values is just as important as passing on your valuables!

How to Begin Giving and Making a Difference

Before giving to a cause, person, or organization, take time to think about the legacy you'd like to leave through your giving, one that lives on after you're no longer living—if that is important to you. Take time to explore your values. What's really important to you?

My husband and I have talked about the gifts we want to leave with our passing. He wants to have a park bench donated in his name in a park high on a hill, where people can take a rest from hiking. I want to donate to special causes near and dear to my heart. Others, like my mom and dad, prefer to give to their children during their lifetime. They've said many times, "We want to see you enjoy it now, not when we're dead."

Here are some ideas that can help you begin your exploration. If you value a higher education, you might think of contributing or creating an educational fund to help someone better afford college. Your financial planner can help you set this up. You can also create a scholarship in your name at your local university and fund it year after year.

Or find a family in your community that needs help. Each season, gift them items that will help make a difference. This could include grocery cards, toys and educational books for the kids, seasonal clothing, and some movie tickets for fun. Little ideas like this create so much joy. Each year we fund a family for the holiday. There is nothing like knowing you helped someone to smile or that you lightened their load, even a little bit.

Make sure the money you give to an organization isn't all eaten up in overhead costs, that the majority of the money goes to the cause at hand and reaches the people in need. A friend of mine sponsors a family in another country, because her American dollars buy a lot more abroad. She's bought the family a cow, sheep, and clothes for three kids to go to school.

Giving keeps the flow going. Money is energy—it comes in and it goes out. It's your job to make sure to use and give it wisely.

Words of Wisdom From Trusted Financial Planners and Advisors

Richard Chambers
CFP®, Founder of Investor's Capital Management

94

A successful financial life should provide for giving. Everyone has favorite charities—plan to give annually, even if the amounts are small at first. If you are inclined, make charities a beneficiary of your estate.

For your long-term financial plan, make this happen: when you are seventy and a half and are required to take a minimum distribution (RMD) from your retirement accounts, give the RMD to charity. It keeps your taxes lower and is a wonderful way to give back in your later years.

Sheryl Garrett
CFP®, AIR®, Founder of the Garrett Planning Network, Inc.

Giving from the heart is part of many people's worldview. It's important to remember you don't have to give with cash; lots of people can write a check. Consider offering your time, talent, and energy to propel the mission of a charity near and dear to your heart, especially if you're working on getting yourself out of debt and trying to meet your retirement financial goals.

Teresa Scagliotti
CFP®, Founder of Scagliotti and Associates Financial Planning

Giving can come in many fashions. It can come in the way of donating funds to organizations with which we have strong allegiances, or it can come in the way of giving back with our time and with our hearts.

Everyone has a different take on how much to give, or even whether to give—this is personal to every individual. First determine whether you desire to give, then whether you can afford to give funds. Giving from the heart can provide an incredible sense of joy and satisfaction, and thus enrich our everyday life.

Hilary Martin

MBA, CFP®, Healthy Wealthy Families

Becoming someone who regularly gives money away was a bit of a transformational experience for me. Once I gave myself permission to give money away, I was no longer allowed to be someone who didn't have enough money. You can only give away what you have when you have enough—when your cup is full— and I had always thought of myself as someone who didn't have enough. So I had to transform that thinking, and that was one of the most generous things I have ever done for myself financially.

Joanna Nowak

MBA, CFP®, Principal, MoneyWise Financial Advisors

People who live their lives to the fullest are committed to purposes much, much bigger than themselves. They give of themselves in different forms: money, expertise, time, attention, etc. In my opinion, giving and being of service to others is the highest form of self-actualization.

Ready, Set, GIVE: Action Items to Put YOU Back in the Driver's Seat of Your Financial Future

Giving is an important act to open up the flow of abundance in your life. Practice the art of giving each day. Begin with non-monetary giving. Notice how you feel when you give freely in this way. Find a way to give back to others. Be creative. Fund a small project first, then grow into bigger philanthropy!

Part 3

YOUR
FINANCIAL
TOOLBOX

YOUR FINANCIAL TOOLBOX

I hope this book has inspired you to move through any fear you might have and to take action in creating your financial future, regardless of what your finances are right now. You CAN DO IT! All you need is clarity, a plan, strategy, support, and a willingness to learn.

In this section you'll find several tools to help you put into practice many of the ideas and suggestions presented in the book. These are additional tools besides the exercises at the end of each chapter for you to use to support forward movement in your financial life.

We'll start with the Financial Assessment Tool, then go on to the Vision Board Tool, the Earnings Tool, the Savings Tool, the Get-Out-of-Debt Tool, and the Gratitude Tool. Pick and choose what tool best supports you along your unique path in creating the life you desire!

My final thought is this: money takes up space in our lives, one way or another. We can live in the shadow with money, worrying about it, having it take up our brain space and be all-consuming when we don't manage our finances. Or we can step into the light with money, be in relationship with it, and give it its due! Either way is a spending of our time—one positive, one negative.

Which experience will you create and choose for yourself?

Financial Assessment Tool

This Financial Health Assessment is a financial self-assessment of you and your relationship with money. It will help make apparent where you need to step into your knowing more and create practices with your money that bring you greater connection with it.

Check "YES" or "NO" for each statement. Statements answered with yes support healthy financial practices. If you answered a statement with no, turn it around with a new behavior and create a healthy financial practice. You can pace yourself, remembering to take baby steps toward your goals.

Healthy Financial Practices (Good Basic Housekeeping)

YES NO

☐ ☐ I open my mail daily and sort my bills from junk mail.

☐ ☐ I pay my bills with gratitude for services I have received by honoring their due date.

☐ ☐ I have an organized financial filing system.

☐ ☐ I have a special space in my home where I manage my finances.

☐ ☐ I am current with payments on all bills and debts.

☐ ☐ I use one method to pay my bills, automated or manual.

☐ ☐ If I pay electronically, I hold the reigns to when money is taken out of my account.

☐ ☐ I know my credit score and it is _____.

☐ ☐ I keep a meticulously clean purse or wallet with cash, coins, and plastic each in their own compartment.

YES   NO

☐   ☐   I know at any given time the exact "real" balance in my checking account.

☐   ☐   I create a cash flow plan every month, plan my spending, and stick to it.

☐   ☐   I track and analyze cash flow in order to stay conscious to choices I make.

☐   ☐   I keep at least $100 on my person just in case I need it.

☐   ☐   I am aware of my net and gross monthly pay and any deductions that are taken out of my paycheck.

☐   ☐   I am free of any credit card debt.

☐   ☐   I keep a cushion of $500-$1000 in my checking account.

☐   ☐   Money flows in my life in this order: Earn, Save, Spend, Give.

Healthy Earning Practices

☐   ☐   I earn to my full potential and know my market value.

☐   ☐   I earn enough to live within my means, save for retirement, and have fun.

☐   ☐   When I get a raise, I sock that money in the bank rather than increase my lifestyle expenses.

☐   ☐   I am comfortable asking for a raise or promotion that supports my level of contribution and performance.

☐   ☐   I am as good a receiver as I am a giver.

Healthy Savings Practices

YES   NO

☐ ☐ I fully fund my seasonal savings account (non-monthly expenses).

☐ ☐ I have an emergency savings to cover six months of living expenses.

☐ ☐ I fully fund my retirement account each year.

☐ ☐ I track the annual rate of return on my investments.

☐ ☐ I know how much money I need saved to retire.

☐ ☐ I am good at delaying gratification.

☐ ☐ I know the difference between saving and investing.

☐ ☐ I review all savings and investment balances each month.

Healthy Spending Practices

☐ ☐ I shop with a list and purchase just what I need.

☐ ☐ I stay away from shopping if I am feeling blue, depressed, angry, hungry, lonely, or tired.

☐ ☐ I spend guilt free with no after effects of regret or remorse.

☐ ☐ I use cash, check, or an ATM debit card when I make purchases.

☐ ☐ I practice funding my "needs" over superficial "wants" and know the difference.

☐ ☐ I save up for big purchases rather than go into debt.

YES NO

☐ ☐ When I spend, I ask myself if the expense gives me fulfillment, satisfaction, and value in proportion to the money I just spent.

☐ ☐ My dollars nourish my deepest values and priorities.

Healthy Giving Practices

☐ ☐ I believe in giving back to things that make a difference in my life.

☐ ☐ I am happy for another's abundance and don't compare myself to others.

☐ ☐ If I was out of work, I would be comfortable telling family and friends I wouldn't be gifting over the holiday.

☐ ☐ I practice daily gratitude and feel joy for all I have been given in my life.

☐ ☐ I understand the difference between healthy giving, enabling, and rescuing.

☐ ☐ I easily choose what I want to give, to whom, when, and how much.

☐ ☐ I don't feel pressured by others' expectations any time of the year.

Healthy Money Mindsets

☐ ☐ When it comes to money, I feel control, peace, and confidence.

☐ ☐ I am good at balancing short- and long-term goals, funding both over time.

YES   NO

☐   ☐   I can easily set priorities and base my spending accordingly.

☐   ☐   I realize money can't buy me happiness. Finding joy is an inside job.

☐   ☐   I am good at seeing unhealthy financial patterns I have and taking action to overcome them.

☐   ☐   I feel competent to create the financial life I desire.

☐   ☐   I consider myself a good steward in how I handle my life resources.

☐   ☐   I set financial goals for myself yearly and meet them.

☐   ☐   I have the power to live the life of my dreams while living within my means.

Vision Board Tool

A vision board is an amazing, fun tool, a visual representation of images that embody your deepest desires and dreams regarding what you want to create in your life. Your job is to get clear on what you want to create, believe your vision is within your reach, and to take action that supports you getting what you desire.

One reason a vision board is so powerful is that it helps us to envision what we want to create, rather than stay in the space where we are. Here's what some of the greats say about visioning and imagining:

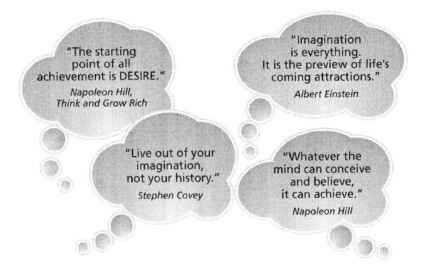

"The starting point of all achievement is DESIRE."
Napoleon Hill,
Think and Grow Rich

"Imagination is everything. It is the preview of life's coming attractions."
Albert Einstein

"Live out of your imagination, not your history."
Stephen Covey

"Whatever the mind can conceive and believe, it can achieve."
Napoleon Hill

Step 1

So, what do you want to *HAVE, BE, or DO?* List it all out right here. Do you want to fully fund your retirement account? Earn more money? Get out of debt? Simplify your lifestyle? Organize your finances? Whatever you desire to create in your financial life in the next year, list it here and realize you are creating a new financial energy template for yourself:

1.

2.

3.

4.

5.

Step 2

Create a digital or handmade board of images that speak to your deepest desires. Place this in a space where you will look at it daily (on your computer, bathroom mirror, etc.). The reason gathering images is so important is that images elicit feelings, and the combination of our feelings + thoughts + actions toward our desires = dreams come true.

Step 3

Stay conscious, now that you have put your intentions out to the Universe via your vision board. Watch for synchronicities in your life that open you to new opportunities—maybe you'll meet someone, or a book will come your way with information you need to move forward. Step through the opportunity—forms of new abundance often come forth from opportunity, such as money, health, relationships, career, etc.

Visioning is a powerful tool. I do vision boards every January and June—namely because the visioning I do in January has all come forth by June of every year. Play with this tool. Dream. Imagine your desires (right-brain mental activity), stay focused, and see what new financial picture you can create for yourself from the inside out!

Earnings Tool: Funding Basic Survival Needs
AKA The Bare Bones Spending Plan

It is important to know how much money you need to earn to pay for your survival needs. This is the minimum amount of money you need to earn to sustain yourself. Once you've figured out your target number, add a percentage for taxes so you'll have an idea of the gross income you need to fund survival needs.

If you know your target survival number, you can begin to use this as your savings goal for the account called "Life's Curveballs."

Monthly Survival Expense	Current Cost	Notes to Self
Rent/Mortgage		
Utilities (heat, water, garbage, electricity)		
Food		
Phone (land line, cell)		
Health Insurance and Vision, Medical, and Dental Out-of-Pocket		
Transportation (car payment, fuel, registration, repairs)		
Grooming (hair, skin, body care)		
Total cost of my survival needs =		

Spending Tool: Identifying Needs

One way to begin to connect more with your true needs is to evaluate which of Glasser's five needs you are meeting when you purchase something. Are you spending to purchase a survival need? Love and Belonging? Freedom? Personal Power? Fun? At first, it might be difficult to identify the need. But by using this form daily, reflecting on the need underneath each purchase you make is going to give you an opportunity to really get connected with why you spend money on the things you do. Make copies of this form and use it daily for one month—and see what you discover about your spending behaviors and the needs you're trying to fulfill.

Month / Date	Expense Purchased	Cost of the Expense	Need Met by the Expense	Notes to Self

Get-Out-of-Debt Tool

1. Gain clarity on exactly how much credit card debt you have, the percentage of interest you are paying on any revolving debt, current debt balances, and your minimum monthly payments. Here's a tool to help you achieve this clarity.

Name of Debt	Annual APR %	Minimum Monthly Payment	Current Balance

2. Unless you're out of work and you place survival needs on a credit card as a temporary measure until you get back to work, draw a mental line in the sand and vow to yourself that you are going to stop going deeper into credit card debt today. Find other creative ways to get your needs met. This won't be easy at first. Using credit cards gives us the illusion we have more money available to spend than we actually do. Take your cards out of your wallet for a first step. Freeze them in your refrigerator freezer. Experiment with how it feels to do life without your credit cards. Most people experience some sort of grieving process, because you have a relationship with your credit cards. They have been your back-up.

3. Consider transferring your credit card debt, if you can, to a lower interest alternative. Sometimes your credit union can help with this. Or you can call and see if your current creditor will lower your interest rate. One of my clients had $75,000 worth of credit card debt and, over a period of years, transferred the debt from her higher interest card to serial 0% credit cards until the debt was entirely paid off.

4. When you pay off one debt, transfer the monthly payment for the paid-off debt to another current debt. Over time, this strategy supports you paying off your debt faster.

5. Decide which debt you will pay off first, second, third, and so on. While financially it makes more sense to pay off the higher interest cards first, emotionally it might make sense to pay off a card with a lower interest rate, if the debt placed on that card reminds you of a difficult time. For example, Joan had a credit card at a lower interest rate, and the debt placed on that card was from her wedding that didn't happen (the groom cancelled at the last minute). Each month when this credit card bill came around, it reminded her of this sad time in her life. So for Joan, this was the debt she wanted to pay off first.

6. If you vow to stop debting and continue to pay off your debts, you will eventually be debt-free.

Something else to think about. In years of working with clients, I have noticed this: it is best to pay off your debt in a slow and steady manner, month after month, rather than all at once. This is behaviorally smart because, as you decrease your debt over time (without incurring new debt), you begin to decrease the experience of deprivation in your life. As you release the energy of deprivation little by little, you simultaneously create a new experience for yourself of abundance. While this may not always be the smartest financial strategy (unless you are paying more than 0% on your credit cards), it is the smartest behavioral strategy. I've witnessed clients using this strategy to stay out of debt permanently, rather than having the yo-yo behavior of going into debt, getting back out, and repeating the cycle over and over.

Gratitude Tool

Each day write down 10 things you are grateful for. Gratitude changes your body's internal chemistry from one of lack to a state of abundance. Living in more moments of gratitude has the possibility of creating for you inside fulfillment, happiness, and a more positive outlook on life!

People, Experiences, Blessings, and Things I Am Grateful for in My Life Today

1. _____

2. _____

3. _____

4. _____

5. _____

6. _____

7. _____

8. _____

9. _____

10. _____

About the Author

Denise Hughes is an inspirational speaker, author, avid hiker, and sought-after financial consultant. *The Wall Street Journal*, *Money Magazine*, *Financial Advisor*, and other prestigious journals seek her advice on matters of love, money, and relationships.

Once on the brink of divorce over money matters in her own marriage, she now consults with couples, individuals, and entrepreneurs on how to make money work in life and business. Denise shares sound advice for gaining control over our finances, "right-sizing" our lives, and living a life of abundance from the inside out.

Denise earned a master's degree in Counseling Psychology at Notre Dame de Namur University, Belmont, California, a certification in Financial Counseling at the Financial Recovery Institute in Marin, California, and a certificate in Interactive Guided Imagery from Beyond Ordinary Nursing.

She currently lives happily in Northern California with her husband, Greg, and two dogs, Sadie and Kiska.

To hire Denise to speak to your organization or to help you create the financial life you desire, visit her website at www.denisehughes.org.